DEAD
BODY
CALLS

Dead Body Calls
LOREN W. CHRISTENSEN

First Edition 2021

ISBN: 9798495496590

Cover and interior design by Kamila Miller kzmiller.com

Disclaimer:
The author has tried to recreate events, locales and conversations to the
best of his recollection. In order to maintain anonymity in some instances
he may have changed or otherwise obscured the names of individuals,
identifying characteristics and details.

DEAD BODY CALLS

One Street Cop's Experiences with
Homicides
Suicides
Fatal Accidents
Natural Deaths

Loren W. Christensen

ACKNOWLEDGEMENTS

A big hug to my wife, Lisa, a passionate UFO researcher,
a keen-eyed editor, and mostly tolerant of my angst.

Kevin Faulk, friend, editor, and a combat
veteran of the war in Afghanistan

My long-time friend Lt. Col. Dave Grossman
for writing the Foreword

Kamila Miller for her always excellent
cover design and interior layout

Table of Contents

Those we love don't go away; they walk beside us every day.
Unheard, unseen, but always near, still
loved, still missed, and very dear.

an Irish poem, unknown author

FOREWORD

by Lt. Col. Dave Grossman

I can speak of Loren Christensen from decades of personal experience. He is a good man, and he has been a true friend and a worthy co-author. He has walked the warrior path throughout his life, seeking the realm of violence and death from his youngest days. I have personally been in awe of him in all of his manifestations and count myself privileged to know him and to work with him.

Perhaps, most of all, Loren has been a prolific and brilliant wordsmith. And this book may be the pinnacle of his craft.

Take this journey with Loren. Let him be your Charon, your ferryman across the River Styx to the land of death. And in doing so, you will explore, prepare for, help make peace with, and make sense of, your own paths and experiences with death, past, present, and future.

Loren will show you how precious every moment and every life can be. How the casual unkindness you inflict upon others, can echo back to haunt you when they are gone. He will tell you of "a friend who would never hear my apology." He can teach you one of life's great lessons: how precious every moment can be, and the need for kindness and gentleness toward every person.

Loren has always been in touch with the supernatural and the paranormal, as can be seen from his bestselling books on the subject. *But the supernatural has also been in touch with Loren.* From his grandfather's funeral, when the rain stopped, a beam of sunlight pierced the clouds, and an earthquake struck. To his "good karma" and chilling "sixth sense" of a pending ambush as a street cop.

I believe, again, it is very clear that the supernatural has been in touch with Loren. Not just in these undeniable incidents, but also in the slow stately flow of his warrior path of life and death, as recorded in this book. He has been gifted with a fierce and gentle soul, and an uncommon gift for crafting the written word. Now, it appears that one of Loren's missions here on Earth, has been to serve as a speaker for the dead. And he has fulfilled his charge, completed his mission, finished that task, with this book.

Loren quite appropriately concludes with this wisdom: "A funeral director's job is one of the most unappreciated professions there is...But it's one of the most valuable ones in our culture."

And so is the eulogist for the forgotten. The speaker for the dead.

So, walk this path with Loren. There is so much to gain, he has so much to teach.

And, when our time comes, if we are to die alone and anonymous in some "tiny flophouse apartment" (as could happen to any of us, when life and death mete out our final portion), may we have the blessing of such a gifted wordsmith, and such a gentle heart, to recognize us in our passing as a fellow human being.

His dedication to the book bears repeating:

Those we love don't go away; they walk beside us every day.

Unheard, unseen, but always near, still
loved, still missed, and very dear.

an Irish poem, unknown author

Dave Grossman, Lt. Col., US Army, retired.

Author of: *On Killing, On Combat* (with Loren W. Christensen), and *On Spiritual Combat*
LT. COL. DAVE GROSSMAN, U.S. Army (ret.)
Director, Killology Research Group
www.killology.com

Lt. Col. Dave Grossman is an award-winning author, and nationally recognized as a powerful, dynamic speaker. He has authored over a dozen books, to include his "perennial bestseller" *On Killing* and a *New York Times* best-selling book co-authored with Glenn Beck. His books are "required" or "recommended" reading in all four branches of the US Armed Forces, and in federal and local law enforcement academies nationwide. His book *On Combat*, co-authored with Loren W. Christensen, has been on the USMC "Commandant's required reading list" since its publication, and as recently as 2021 it has appeared as Amazon's #1 Best Seller in several categories.

Grossman is a US Army Ranger, a paratrooper, a prior service sergeant, and a former West Point Psychology Professor. He has five patents to his name, has earned a Black Belt in *Hojutsu* (the martial art of the firearm), and has been inducted into the USA Martial Arts Hall of Fame.

His research was cited by the President of the United States in a national address, he has testified before the U.S. Senate, the U.S. Congress, and numerous state legislatures, and has been invited to the White House on two occasions to brief the President and the Vice President in his areas of expertise.

Since his retirement from the US Army in 1998, he has been on the road over 200 days a year, for over 24 years, as one of our nation's leading trainers for military, law enforcement, mental health providers, and school safety organizations. He been inducted as a "Life Diplomate" by the American Board for Certification in Homeland Security, and a "Life Member" of the American College of Forensic Examiners Institute.

INTRODUCTION

I don't recall how aware I was of death before my grandfather died when I was 12. I saw it in the movies and on television, and I played war and cowboys and Indians with my friends, slaughtering one another in our backyards. I was aware of it in my early teens because I watched the news. I was a junior in high school when John Kennedy was assassinated on November 22, 1963. Two days later, I watched Lee Harvey Oswald take a fatal bullet on TV. That was a crash course in death.

Here are my early experiences with death that affected me on a personal level. Little did I know, there would be so many more.

The first

The service for my grandfather was on a rainy weekday in Salem, Oregon. I don't remember anything about what happened inside the church, nor do I remember whether it was an open-casket service. If I had to guess based on how my father viewed death, it was closed. I remember the gravesite service vividly, helped by a photo of the Christensen men standing by the open hole; I was wearing a snazzy suit and a fedora hat.

It was raining steadily, and the group of us were huddled under umbrellas around the coffin. I had never seen my dad cry, and I was as unsettled seeing that as I was of the proceedings. But nothing could prepare me for what happened next.

When everyone had said their goodbyes to my grandfather, the coffin began to descend to its final resting place. That's when three things happened, one after the other.

The rain that had not let up all day, abruptly stopped.

A ray of sunshine found its way through the tall trees to fall on the gathering like a heavenly stage light.

The ground trembled hard. An earthquake.

I squatted to touch the ground to keep my balance. Others startle-yelped as they shuffled about to stay on their feet, and some oohed and aahed then nervously laughed. My dad was one of the laughers as he simultaneously wept and knuckled tears from his cheeks.

Driving home, my dad didn't place any significance on the chain of events other than to shake his head and say, "Wasn't that something?" I thought that was an understatement since, in my mind, earthquakes only happened to big-name people who died in the Bible.

I didn't know what I thought of it in my 12-year-old head. Coincidental? A religious miracle?

I rarely saw my grandfather, though he lived in the same town. I can only assume he and my father had a strained relationship. My mother often spoke of him as being cruel, but I never knew in what way. I believe she didn't like him since she didn't go to the funeral.

She missed a heck of a show.

The second

John Zimmer drowned when we were both 16. He lived two blocks away, but he didn't hang around much with my neighborhood buddies. John was the same age as us but matured faster. He smoked in his mid-teens, rode in cars with older guys, and fished with a couple of tough-looking guys I'd seen around and always avoided.

He drowned with them one hot day in June.

They were in a rowboat on Vancouver Lake, about four miles west of my home in Vancouver, Washington. None of the three survived to explain what happened. The press blamed their waders, those rubber suits fishermen wear to shield them from the wet and cold. The boat flipped, the press assumed, the waders filled up, and the three sunk.

It was a strange feeling to know that a kid died I had gone to school with since fourth grade, played with when we were younger, and who lived just a few blocks away. I didn't yet know the expression "facing one's own mortality," but I could feel it. I was 16, and so was John.

Now he was dead.

Death suddenly seemed frighteningly real, unexpected, and cruel.

The third

Howard was the first in our group to go into the service. I had known him since fourth grade. He was shorter than the rest of us with an unruly mop of dirty blond hair and a little slow on the uptake, which made him the butt of our relentless teasing. Whatever went on in his house caused him to stutter around his old man but never around us. When Howard left for the airport to fly to Vietnam, he told his dad, "I'm not coming back."

Less than a month later, my mother greeted me at the door as I returned from work and told me to sit down. She had just received a call from a neighbor—Howard had been killed. He had been based on some nameless hill when a Viet Cong rocket attack slammed into his camp, killing him and many others.

My mother told me later that when she gave me the news, my head had snapped back. All I remember of that moment was sinking deeper and deeper into my chair as her words repeated in my brain: "Howard was killed. Howard was killed. Howard was…"

A few weeks earlier, I had embarrassed him.

He had been home on leave from the Marines, looking sharp in his uniform, taller, older, and more mature. All the gang met at Richard's house to drink beer and listen to Howard's stories of his first few months in the Corps.

Although he had always been the smallest of our group and the butt of our practical jokes, he preferred being around us to being home with his father. I'm sure he hadn't forgotten the loving yet rough treatment he had received from us growing up, but now he was enjoying admiration from the same guys who had barely matured at all.

At one point, he told us about his hand-to-hand training and how he had developed a skill level to destroy anyone foolish enough to attack him. I had studied karate for two years at that point, and I was working hard for the coveted brown belt. I was 20 years old, cocky, and full of myself.

I piped up that I had been training four days a week for two years, so there was no way his eight hours of training could match a karate man's techniques. I told Howard the service brainwashed him. I said I had read an article about how Marine boot camp was all about convincing impressionable young men that they were unbeatable.

Howard's face reddened, and he jabbed his finger at me. "My techniques are for killing," he said. "They are better than what you've been learning."

I jumped up. "Okay, show me one of your *killing techniques.*'" He got into a corny stance that actors at the time used when pretending to know karate. I assumed my stance and waited. He lunged forward with a punch; I blocked it, swept his feet out from under him, and down he went.

Everyone roared with laughter at how Howard had fallen. Suddenly, we were all 14-years old again, and once more, the runt in our group had been the victim of roughhousing. Howard, his face crimson, leaped to his feet and angrily dusted himself off. He wasn't physically hurt, but there was a pain in his eyes as he looked at each one of us. I, however, felt good because I had shown the superiority of karate—and my superiority. His embarrassment was irrelevant because it was only Howard, just as it was "only Howard" when we had tormented him for so many years. A few minutes later, he quietly slipped on his coat, grimly shook hands with everyone, and left.

Three weeks later, a Viet Cong rocket snuffed his life.

In time, I would realize the issue that night wasn't my karate training vs. his Marine training. The fact was, I had felt threatened by Howard. He had gone away, and his experiences and training had made him grow and mature far more than I. He had moved beyond our neighborhood group, and I was still there, feeling stagnant. Because of my immaturity and lack of confidence, I had to show him I was still his superior—and I needed to convince myself too.

The more I thought about it in the days after his death, the more I realized I was not an expert in the martial arts as I had thought. I still had a long way to go and much to learn. Sadly, I had embarrassed a friend in the process.

A friend who would never hear my apology.

The fourth

Two years later, I was in Vietnam as a military policeman. I felt death's presence the moment I stepped out of the jet at 1 a.m., along with the wilting heat and humidity. I heard artillery—ours, theirs, I didn't know—pounding the earth, lighting the horizon, and no doubt turning people into a fine, red mist.

A week later, I was assigned to the 716th MPs in Saigon, ranked then as "The most dangerous city in the world," and given a bunk where a pile of Army fatigues lay neatly folded. They belonged to two MPs killed a few days earlier, Eugene Cox and James Workman. Was I their replacement?

I was too overwhelmed by this new world to yet process the mad assault of sights, sounds, and information bombarding me. But not so overcome that I couldn't feel the chills goosebump my skin as I looked at those clothes.

I tell their story later.

Two years after I got home from the war, I joined the Portland Police Bureau in Oregon. As a street cop, there were times I was getting so many dead body calls that other officers teasingly called me the "Death Car." Additionally, the morgue was in our beat, which meant my partner and I were often called there to identify freshly brought in corpses without identification.

This book tells of my experiences with the victims of suicide, homicide, fatal accidents, and natural deaths that crossed my path.

I show the effect that the deaths had on family and friends at the scenes, and I reflect on how some sights left a mental imprint I still feel and see in my mind's eye years later.

I respected the many victims I encountered and the responsibility I had as the cop on the scene. I have made every effort not to present these stories in a gratuitous and salacious manner. My objective is to show one aspect of the police job that officers do thousands of times a year.

On The Writing

I have broken my experiences into four sections: Murder, Fatal Accidents, Suicides, and Natural Deaths. While most of the stories occurred during my 25-year career as a police officer in Portland, Oregon, some sections begin with one or more incidents from my time as a military policeman in Saigon, Vietnam, 1969-1970. I include these because they were among my first exposure to the deceased.

Names of victims, officers, other participants, and specific locations in the city have been changed.

SECTION ONE

HOMICIDE

It's easier to commit murder than to justify it, someone said. This was true in my experience.

I wrote an article once about two detective partners in the Portland Police Bureau's Homicide Unit who had just investigated their 100th murder. One hundred! They went on to work many more cases before they retired. The three of us agreed that so many killings are difficult, if not impossible, to justify to those not involved in their situation.

Here is an example of a case with an absurd justification that didn't end up in murder, but it could have. It involves a Southeast Asian gang member, a high school student.

The bell rang, indicating it was time for students to leave their present class and move to their next. The gangbanger, his books tucked under his arm, was walking down the hall with other students when he locked eyes with a kid coming his way. As they closed the space between them, the other kid "looked at me with disrespect," the suspect would later say.

Maybe the look was a frown, a glare, or a hard stare. Or all three. In street gang parlance, such a look is called "dissin'." In this case, the gangbanger thought the other kid's facial expression indicated he was deliberately disrespecting him.

Enraged by the dissin', the gangbanger left the school and walked two blocks to an Asian grocery where he bought a large meat cleaver. The gangbanger went back to his high school, searched for the disser, found him, and chopped a large wedge of meat and tendons from his shoulder. Was he aiming for the kid's neck a few inches higher? He didn't admit to it, but I'd bet he was based on my years working street gang intelligence.

His need for revenge completed, he cleaned the blade and walked back to the store. He told the storekeeper he didn't need the chopper after all and got his money back.

I think most rational people would find this act, attempted murder, hard to justify.

In another case, also involving gangbangers, one member met another for the first time. Within a few minutes, one felt he was being disrespected and shot the other one dead.

Sadly, most gang officers have stories similar to this.

The two homicide detectives I interviewed said most of their cases were the result of lifestyle, such as people involved in street gangs, hanging out in tough bars, running with a rough crowd, engaging in selling and buying illegal narcotics, prostituting themselves on the mean streets, and participating in other felonious crimes. Yes, people have a right to live the way they want, but there is a risk.

A WORD ABOUT HOMICIDE BY FIREARMS

Big city cops respond to a lot of shootings. As I write this, the morning news reported that 104 people were shot in Chicago over the weekend, including a 6-year-old girl and two police officers. New York City had a little under that number. Nationwide, there were more than 400 shootings, dozens killed on the same weekend. Last Saturday, six people were shot in my town, one fatally. Less than a week later, a rapper named KZTS Dre was released from a Chicago jail. He hadn't even reached the car that was to drive him away when suspects bailed out of two vehicles and began shooting the man. By the time it was over, the victim had been hit 64 times. Ironically, the rapper had a gun target tattooed on his neck.

Mass shootings—defined as shootings involving four or more people—are increasing at an alarming rate. In fact, they no longer get the press they once did, and when they do, it quickly disappears from the lead story.

Shots ring out, 911 is called, and cops respond to the epidemic. A shooting call instantly floods the officer's system with adrenalin, heightening their alertness and awareness. The callers to 911 are almost always hysterical, under the influence of adrenaline and shock, all of which can distort their perception.

Sometimes callers to 911 scream into their phone, "Someone's shot!" and hang up. When officers are given limited and erroneous information, they must enter a volatile scene where the participants and witnesses are in a mental zone of out-of-control emotions and sound decision-making.

Most of the shooting scenes I walked into were total chaos—people screaming, crying, shouting, and fighting. And they expected the just-arrived cops to instantly know what was happening, understand who the players were, and get everything under control in a nanosecond.

Sometimes two people in the front yard would shout simultaneously, "That's the guy who did it," as they pointed at each other. Or people screamed at the officer to "Stop that car! The driver shot my cousin." But at the same time, another person was jabbing his finger at someone darting off between two houses shouting, "No, that's the shooter right there. Go after him!"

When there was a bloody body, the officer had to decide whether to tend to the victim or first check the hostile crowd for the shooter. If the suspect was present, the officer had to determine if he was still armed. This was a high risk since the police presence might have triggered the desperate shooter to use his weapon again to make his getaway. This most often took place in the midst of agitated, volatile, and violent people.

My fellow officers and I have been in these kinds of chaotic scenes many times. And, at least for me, they never got easier.

CHAPTER 1

Saigon, Vietnam
Cox and Workman

Another military policeman helped me carry my gear up to my sleeping quarters in the 716th MP Battalion in Saigon, Vietnam. I'd been in-country for about five days.

We dumped my duffle bag and my newly acquired flack vest and steel helmet on the floor just inside the door. A large, shuttered window looked out on a busy street, my introduction to the insanity of Saigon's traffic. When I turned around to check out the room further, I noticed two neat stacks of fatigues and vests by the door. The name tags on the shirts read Cox and Workman.

"Someone storing their stuff here?" I asked, walking over to check out the bunk. When the man didn't answer, I turned around to see if he had left. He was still there, standing over the two piles, his shoulders slumped.

"Eugene Cox and James Workman were both killed last week," he said softly.

I looked at him. "They were ..."

"MPs. Killed. Shot. They responded to a drunken soldier in a bar and were shot dead by a South Vietnamese Lieutenant Colonel. Turns out the shooter was the son of a high-ranking Vietnamese police official. I don't think anything is going to happen to him."

I learned that the MPs were working a combined patrol— American MPs, Vietnamese Army MPs, and Vietnamese civilian police. As I would do hundreds of times during my year there, they responded to a disturbance at a bar. But within minutes of their entry, there was an explosion of gunfire, and Cox and Workman were slain. The suspect was a much-decorated Vietnamese officer, the brother of a South Vietnamese Army General.

In the months that followed, politics, legal wrangling, denial, and accusations were the stuff of a suspenseful Hollywood movie. In the end, neither the killer nor his associates that night were charged.

All walked free.

I looked at their gear for the next two days as I passed in and out of my room. The ranks on their shirts indicated they were specialist 4th class, the same as me. On the third day, the uniforms were gone.

Death had been talked about nonstop since I had joined the Army two years earlier. Seeing these piles of personal gear represented two young MPs who had been doing their tour, counting the days before they would go home (they both had a month left). They responded to a call, just as I would soon be doing, and within minutes they were gone. Dead.

The first week I was in Vietnam, I had been repeatedly greeted with, "Welcome to the 'Nam, Christensen."

Every time I passed the uniforms, I would glance at them and read the names on the shirts. It would scare me, piss me off, and fill me with dread.

Welcome to the 'Nam, Christensen.

CHAPTER 2

Saigon, Vietnam
Dead Mamasan

The shot-dead middle-aged Vietnamese woman lay face-up on the dock.

She was wearing the typical white blouse and black silk pants, though the blouse was blood-soaked. A halo of red pooled about her head. Her sun-damaged face and thick, calloused hands revealed years of hard work. Blood-red water slopped about in the bottom of a rowboat tied to the dock a few feet away. Seventy-five yards away, a grey Vietnamese ship sat anchored; on the deck, dozens of faces too far away to see clearly, looked our way.

My partner and I positioned ourselves to watch the half dozen Vietnamese that had gathered on the dock. Any one of them could be the shooter. Since this was a Vietnamese civilian matter, we didn't have any say in the investigation unless we were asked by the *cahn sats,* the Vietnamese civilian police, to assist in some way. So, we simply stood by and watched with suspicious eyes.

About 30 minutes later, the lead *cahn sat* came over and filled us in.

According to witnesses the Vietnamese dispatch talked to the woman had approached the ship in her small boat. When she got too close, someone onboard warned her over a loudspeaker to stay back. They were rightfully concerned she might be trying to plant an explosive charge on the side of the ship.

But instead of heeding the warning, the little boat kept approaching. So, someone on the ship fired into the air. When the woman still didn't stop, the shooter fired again, this time into the water near the boat. Still, she approached. The next shot was aimed as close as possible to the little boat without hitting it.

But it did.

The round struck the metal edge and, according to investigators, kissed off and flipped end-over-end into the woman's neck.

Suuuure, that's what happened, my suspicious brain thought. At that point, I would have put my meager salary on the shooter simply sending a "warning shot" into the woman's body.

One of the *cahn sats* asked my partner and me to lift her torso a little, so he could get a full-body and head photograph. It was unclear why he didn't straddle the woman to capture her face, as I would do years later as a city cop, and then take a second pic to include all her body. But we went along with it because that's what he wanted.

We kneeled behind her, each of us taking a shoulder, and lifted.

Her torso came up, but her head flopped backward until the top of it slapped against her spine. The front of her neck had been blown away—skin, windpipe, and tendons—leaving her head attached only by a section of flesh and one remaining tendon.

Was she shot by a larger caliber than the M-16 the *cahn sats* were told? I'm no expert on bullets, especially ricocheting ones, but I was suspicious. The Vietnamese police and the ARVNs were convinced a ricocheting M-16 round could do such damage when flipping end-over-end.

———————

The woman might have been a VC or sympathizer wanting to damage the ship. Or perhaps she was the innocent victim of an overzealous young man with a bad warning shot. It was also possible that the *cahn sats,* not known for their strong work ethic, were blowing off a homicide.

As I noted earlier, as American MPs, we were powerless to intercede in a Vietnamese case.

So I was left to ponder how just minutes earlier she had been alive and in her boat, but now she lay on an old wooden dock, her sightless eyes facing the blazing Vietnam sun.

I was shocked how her head rolled back until it was stopped by her back. So stunned I, especially given my proximity to her. The woman's head wasn't supposed to roll that far back. In future cases, a human wasn't supposed to be crushed completely flat. A dead baby wasn't supposed to be in a dresser drawer. A man's mouth wasn't supposed to be blown off his face. But at the time, this was my first experience with mutilation.

While the image of the mamasan's head remains with me today, it doesn't bother me. Time and too many other godawful sights have dulled its impact.

There was something else I saw and heard that day that has remained, as well.

First was the sight of the woman's rowboat bobbing in the undulating water a few feet away from where she lay. I don't know why it was nearly half full of water. Perhaps one of the "warning shots" hit under the waterline, as well as the one that impacted the metal edge, sending a bullet end-over-end into her neck—if that's what really happened.

The one through the neck severed a large artery causing the woman to bleed excessively into the boat, rapidly filling with water. By the time it had been towed to the dock in the choppy river, it was half-filled, the liquid crimson and partially covering the dead woman.

The sound is the second thing that has remained with me. The entire time we were on the dock, that little rowboat bobbed, the bloody water inside—*slop…slop*, back and forth, back and forth…

CHAPTER 3

Portland
A Deadly Family Fight

It was my second night on the street out of the Portland Police Academy. I was a rookie, though a year and a half earlier, I had been a military policeman in Saigon, Vietnam. The job was new to me, but violence wasn't.

Dispatch sent my coach and me and three other police units to a shooting, one person down, ambulance on the way. The location was a two-story home.

We pulled to the curb one house down from the location as other police units, marked and unmarked, skidded to a stop every which way in the street. We ran up onto the porch, guns drawn, other officers in front of us, some following close behind. The smell of gun smoke wafted out the front door.

The sights and sounds in the living room were at stimulus overload. Someone had turned the television volume all the way up, the blare tangible. Still, I could hear two women screaming, one bleeding from her head, as officers wrestled a 12-gauge shotgun out of a teenage boy's hands. They quickly forced him to the floor on his belly and handcuffed him.

More people appeared from somewhere, and commenced shouting, crying. They must have been neighbors or other family members who someone had called to the house. A senior officer ordered officers to block all entrances to the home.

My coach was busy trying to calm the bleeding woman. Since the living room was getting so crowded, and I didn't know what I was supposed to be doing, I moved into a hallway to the left of the living room. A man lay on his back halfway down it, his legs sprawled awkwardly and his head in a wide circle of blood; his expression was that of surprise.

There was a large splash of blood on his shirt over his heart. We would learn it was the entrance wound; the one on his back was much larger. I moved back toward the hallway entrance to guard and protect the scene.

When I looked back at the body, I noticed an inch diameter circle on the floor every three feet or so right up to where I was standing. I lifted my foot to see if I had stepped on something.

I found a chunk of bloody-red meat on the sole of my shoe. What the hell?

Two ambulance EMTs rushed by me and dropped to their knees by the body. (EMTs aren't allowed into a violent scene until police officers establish control.) They checked the man's vitals, looked at the entrance wound and the much larger exit hole in his back. Considering the large burrow right through the heart, they didn't try resuscitation.

"Can you guys check something for me?" I asked as they stood. "I have something on the bottom of my shoe."

The closest EMT looked and said without hesitation, "It's an aorta."

"What?" I probably shouted it. "From a heart? This guy's?"

The other EMT gave it an experienced glance. "Yup, an aorta. From the victim here. I heard one of the officers say the shotgun was loaded with slugs. The big round must have blown the aorta right out of him."

The EMT kindly pried it from the sole of my shoe.

Since it was our call, my coach and I took the kid into custody, placed him into the backseat of our car, and hauled him to the Detective's Division to be interviewed.

We would learn that the boy was 16 years old. The bleeding woman was his mother and the newly deceased man his stepfather. The stepfather had been beating the boy's mother, as he often did, but this time he used a glass ashtray to smash against her head. The son had had enough and retrieved the shotgun from a living room closet. He fired once, one big round right through his stepfather's heart.

The boy had a unique name. Several years later, I heard dispatch send a car to the scene of a violent assault with the suspect last seen running between the neighborhood houses. The dispatcher gave the assailant's name.

It was our shooter, all grown up now.

My first week on the job was intense. I was assigned one of the most active and violent beats in the city. It began with the homicide. A day or two later, we were sent to a car that had plunged into a slough. It had landed upside down with only a single tire protruding out of the water to indicate where it had submerged.

The week ended with a family fight call. The husband stood blocking the doorway, insisting that everything was okay and apologizing that we had to come for nothing. At one point, he moved a couple of inches to the one side, just enough for us to see his wife sitting in an easy chair, a large kitchen knife sticking out from her neck. The husband was a large and powerful man. He resisted so violently that we nearly leveled the house before we could get him into handcuffs.

The wife miraculously survived—then bailed her hubby out of jail.

Even with my experience policing Saigon, the violence and being new on the job were overwhelming. I thought of my academy mates and wondered how they were holding up.

A few years later, I had a trainee who had just graduated from college with a master's in sociology. Our first night together was busy with armed robberies, a family fight where we had to use force to make an arrest, and two bar fights that banged around some.

On the way back to the precinct, my rookie shook his head and said, "They didn't teach me anything about this in college. I had no clue people were so crazy, so quick to act violently."

I wasn't naïve to the human condition when I began working the streets. From my time as an MP, I knew that people could be violent, cruel, and compassionless. And I knew what blood and guts looked and smelled like.

Still, I felt overwhelmed because whoever assigned rookies to the street gave me one of the busiest beats in the city. It was as if I were parachuted into the middle of chaos with an incredible volume of department rules and procedures to follow as well as city and state laws to enforce.

I thank my coach for his guidance and patience.

CHAPTER 4

Death Of A Police Officer

I'd been out of the academy about a month, working the street in North Precinct, when my coach and I stopped for lunch at a burger joint. Another officer joined us, whom I'll call Al Thompson.

Al had been hired a year before me, a personable man who was genuinely interested in me. Rookies weren't always treated kindly when I was hired in 1972, so it was refreshing to be treated with respect. For some reason, I remember Al just having a piece of pie.

One week later, he would be dead.

What follows is the account of what happened as noted at the bureau's Police Museum. I've changed the officer's name to Al Thompson here as well.

"On September 23, 1973, an officer saw a young male driver making "acceleration skids" with his vehicle near SE 18th and Tacoma Street. When the officer attempted to make contact, the man sped away, followed by the patrolman. Soon two more patrol cars joined the pursuit, including one driven by Officer Al Thompson. Several collisions occurred between the patrol cars and the suspect vehicle as it sped alongside streets and onto I-5 northbound.

"Near Killingsworth, the three patrol cars attempted to box in the vehicle. Instead, the driver forced Thompson into a freeway divider just below the Alberta overpass. The suspect's vehicle went out of control and hit the other two cars before coming to a halt. Officer Thompson was killed at the scene, and his partner suffered minor injuries. The 18-year-old suspect was charged with murder.

"Officer Thompson was 30 and survived by his wife."

During my 12-month tour in Vietnam working as a military policeman in Saigon, no MPs were killed in my unit. Two had been killed a couple of weeks before I arrived, which I talked about in Chapter 1, "Cox and Workman."

A year before, in late January 1968, during the lunar new year—commonly called "Tet,"—North Vietnamese and the Viet Cong launched a coordinated attack against 100 cities and outposts in South Vietnam. The U.S. and South Vietnamese militaries sustained heavy losses before finally repelling the assault.

My company lost 27 MPS, many of which I had attended MP School with at Fort Gordon, Georgia. This was devastating news to get my first few days in Vietnam.

Two years later, Al Thompson, a nice man with whom I had just had lunch, perished in a chase.

I didn't have a choice in Vietnam. I had been sent there to the job for which I had trained. The Army didn't care if I was shocked about the loss or stunned to find the uniforms of two recently slain MPS in my sleeping quarters.

However, I had a choice as a civilian police officer. I could quit and do something else, but the thought never crossed my mind, not once. Still, Al Thompson's death chilled me, as it did all the other officers.

Three or four days later, our sergeant told my coach and me to go to the tow lot where Officer Thompson's vehicle had been taken to look for something inside. I no longer recall what it was. It might have been the officer's possessions, paperwork, or something else.

The police car's exterior was crushed and twisted, but it was the interior...

I won't go into the details, but it was apparent the young officer's death was a horrific one. I don't remember how much time the 18-year-old killer got in prison, but it was probably just a little more than what he would get in today's political climate, especially in Portland, Oregon. Two years after Officer Thompson's death, my trainee was shot in the mouth. The shooter served 2 ½ years.

Around this time, I read a story in the newspaper about a murderer getting sentenced to three years in prison. On the same page, an article reported on a tax evader who got sent to the joint for 10.

What are you going to do? It's the only "justice" system we got.

CHAPTER 5

Murder In A High-Rise

My partner and I were working skid row when dispatch broadcasted that a man with a shotgun was roaming the 16th floor of a high-rise. The building was about a mile into the business section of the city. It was noon.

Thirty seconds later, dispatch informed all responding cars that the man had fired several shots. As we neared the structure, dispatch updated us again with this, *"One dead, possibly other injuries. The shooter is a white male, about 40 years, still has the shotgun, and is still walking around on the 16th floor."*

The high-rise was a magnificent structure on the south side of the city. Multiple stories high, it was a solid black structure that emanated power and just a little menace. It had exterior escalators that led up to one of the entrance points. As a half dozen of us rode Code 3 up to the front of the building, people were running down the escalators, some of them screaming, bumping into each other, falling.

As cops do all over the country every day, we ran toward the violence as everyone else streamed past us to safety. Inside the lobby, my partner and I entered an elevator with two other officers and two EMTs. As we rose to the 16th floor, the senior officer said he and his partner would cut to the right when the doors opened and that my partner and I should go left. He told the ambulance people to stay in the elevator until we had control of the scene.

It was a silent ride because we had all turned down our radios to not announce our arrival. We watched the lit floor numbers increase, glanced at one another, then looked back at the numbers again. As we neared the 16th floor, we heard shouting, lots of it.

The doors swished open to pandemonium: people running helter-skelter, crying, and screaming. My partner and I peeled to the left, and the other officers went right. A man streaked around a corner and ran all-out toward my partner and me. "He killed him!" he shouted. "He killed Dr. Johnson!" I asked him where the shooter was. He turned and jabbed his finger toward a set of double doors at the end of the hallway. "In there! He killed him!" With that, he ran off down the hall.

The other two officers heard the man and followed us down the hall toward the French doors, our weapons drawn. A short hallway branched off to the right of the double doors. A door opened halfway down it. The four of us turned as one, our guns pointed at the opening. A white-haired middle-aged woman stuck her head out, saw us, and quickly pulled her head back and shut the door. We turned our attention back to the set of double doors.

I stood to the back end of the right one as the senior officer's partner slowly turned the knob. It opened toward me, which meant I couldn't see in, but I could the officer's face. Her eyes widened as she thrust her weapon forward.

"Drop the gun!" she shouted. "Do it. Drop the gun, or I'll shoot you." I moved around the door opening, taking a position by her side.

The stocky, mid-40s man was dotted with blood, his face, neck, and chest, the shotgun in his hand pointed our way but angled slightly downward. The blood dots were indicators of blow-back, which occurs when a weapon has been discharged within inches of a human target. The man's eyes looked crazed, his mouth moving soundlessly.

With my gun pointed at his face, I took two quick steps, jammed his arm to keep the shotgun pointed down, and swept his feet out from under him. He landed hard. The other officer and I snatched the gun away from him and handed it off to a third officer. We rolled him onto his belly, and with some struggle, managed to get the man handcuffed.

Unbeknownst to me, the senior officer had gone into the other offices, reappearing with a blood-spattered woman. We learned later that she was the victim's secretary and had been taking dictation when the gunman burst into his office and emptied his shotgun into the man's face. He reloaded and fired three more times into him.

The senior officer was a big man, a veteran of witnessing all possible abominations humans can inflict on one another. His face was pale when we first saw him come out from the back. Now it was completely white.

"Don't go in there," he said to us. "You don't want to see that. His head is…"

All the while we searched the gunman, he kept muttering over and over, "I am the extreme executioner of the universe. I am the extreme…" We found another dozen shotgun shells in his pockets.

The double doors were still open, and I saw office workers and TV news cameras all jockeying for position to see what was going on. More officers quickly showed up and managed to push the crowd back so my partner and I could get the suspect to the closest elevator. Ideally, we would have taken him to the basement to stuff him into our car out of the eye of the public and cameras. But in our haste, we had parked in front of the building.

Fortunately, few citizens were near our car, but one TV news crew had staked it out. Considering all the police cars on the scene, someone in the media had a sixth sense that it would be us bringing the man down. The pic of the blood-splattered shooter appeared on the front page of *The Oregonian* the following day.

I'm not much of a drinker, but I wanted to that night. The other closely involved officers did knock back a couple of beers, but I had to teach at my martial arts school. As it turned out, I pushed myself to the brink in class and went home exhausted but feeling better than I would have with a hangover.

The next day, I worked alone. The senior officer from the day before, also working alone, got a call on a violent person acting out in the hallway of a downtown high-rise, and I got the backup. We pulled up to the building at the same time and hurried in.

The ride to the 15th floor in the elevator was as tense as it was 24 hours earlier as we rode to the 16th floor of the other building. We exited the same way, he went right, and I went left. At the end of the hall on my side—another set of double doors.

Dispatch contacted us just then and said witnesses reported the suspect had left the building. The other officer and I looked at each other and simultaneously exhaled.

*

The senior officer and I talked about it a few weeks later, admitting that we had the jitters going into high-rises for a while. We also concurred that entering a similarly styled building the very next day to look for a violent subject was the cherry on our stress with whipping cream.

My anxiety around high-rises lingered, then eventually lessened, though it never went entirely away. Today, I can go into a high-rise without thinking about it. But should I get off an elevator and see a set of French doors at the end of the hall, I hear a whisper: *Remember this?*

Some might wonder why I didn't shoot the guy. When a gun barrel is pointing in your direction but angled down, lifting it and firing takes a nanosecond. Could we have legally shot him? Yes. Were we heroes for not shooting? Absolutely not. I don't know what went through the other officer's mind, but I made a split-second decision to physically take him down. I didn't have a passing thought that I couldn't pull the trigger because I could have. I just reacted, albeit with the serious end of my gun pointed at his medulla oblongata.

It worked. Would I try that again? I don't know. There are too many variables in high-risk scenarios to determine responses in advance.

If only police critics understood this.

CHAPTER 6

Death Of My Training Coach

By the time my probationary training transfers took me to Portland's downtown Precinct, I had been on the job for over a year. My new coach, Nick Meyers, worked upper Northwest, an old neighborhood popular during the hippy era just a few years earlier. There were still a few "long hairs" around, but the neighborhood vibe was changing to one favored by the "look at me" trendy crowd.

Nick and I clicked from the get-go. After teaching me about the area and filling me in on some local bad actors, we became more like partners than training coach and student. I spent four months at Central then transferred to East Precinct to finish my probation.

After a couple of years at East, I got my first trainee, Dale (see his story in Chapter 19, "Shot Trainee"). Though it was a large police agency with lots of training coaches, Dale's first coach was also Nick Meyers.

The various precincts were on different dispatch channels. Usually, officers didn't know what was happening in other precincts unless a situation overlapped, such as a car chase crossing boundaries. Another reason was when a significant incident occurred in one precinct and dispatch determined it was necessary to inform others. Such was the case on the night of the following incident.

Dispatch blared the alert tone, a nerve-igniting sound that forced officers everywhere to stop what they were doing to listen.

Code Zero, Code Zero, two officers down Northwest Twentieth and Kellogg. All units respond.

A call for Code Zero ordered all police officers—uniformed, detectives, undercover, supervisors, Juveniles officers, fingerprint people, and county deputies—to respond lights-and-sirens.

We were on the opposite side of the Willamette River, working a burglary call at the far end of our beat. I had a feeling we would be canceled before we got there. Still, I told Dale to hit the siren and buckle up.

Five minutes later, and just as we were nearing one of the bridges to cross into downtown, we were canceled.

All units not arrived at Twentieth and Kellogg stand down and resume regular patrol. We have enough officers on the scene.

We shut off our lights and siren and headed back to our regular beat, wondering what had happened in Northwest. It had been a busy night, and Dale and I had been racing from call to call. Since several Eastside cars had remained at the Code Zero, we were not only taking our calls but now we were theirs too.

A detective backed us up at a bar fight and afterward asked if we heard what had happened in Northwest. We said all we knew was that two officers were down.

"Right," he said. "Two uniformed guys, one didn't make it."

Dale and I looked at him. After a long moment, I asked who they were. He told us the name of the wounded officer, who I remembered from working downtown. A good officer with a sense of humor that kept all the other cops laughing.

Dale asked, "Who—?" He told me later he had a gut feeling.

"Nick Meyers was killed."

Dale and I both gasped. Our coach.

"You guys knew him?" I nodded, unable to speak. Dale didn't say anything. "Sorry, guys. Hang in there. Sad damn day."

We sat there numb for a few minutes before dispatch interrupted our stupor.

All Southeast units respond to a large brawl in the street at Fiftieth and Center. There's approximately eighty people involved.

By the time we got there, the first officers on the scene had arrested a few people, and the situation was somewhat under control. A multiple-home drinking party had turned ugly, and because there wasn't enough room to fight inside, all the drunks had spilled onto the streets and sidewalks to punch one another.

I had just stepped out of the car when a 20-something man ran up to me screaming, "I just heard a cop got killed tonight." He faked an ugly laugh, adding, "F... him and f... you! I hope all of you cops—" He never finished because I knocked him across the sidewalk and down onto someone's lawn.

I pulled off my badge and dropped it on the sidewalk, muttering something like, "I resign for a few minutes." Then I began to unleash on him. But I didn't get far because other cops grabbed me from behind and pulled me over to our car to chill. I stood there like an obedient child while officers talked to the guy. Just as I was wondering how many days off without pay my captain would give me, the obnoxious man came over and apologized. I accepted it and apologized for knocking him down. We nodded, and that was that.

Here is how the shooting went down. The description is from the Portland Police Museum with minor editing, including calling the victim officer Nick Meyers.

"On August 9, 1974, a [be-on-the] lookout call was issued for a vehicle believed to be driven by an armed robbery suspect. About 8:00 pm, officer Meyers stopped the vehicle... A moment later, a backup officer, Richard James, arrived.

"Meyers got the suspect out of the car at gunpoint and told him he was under arrest. He approached to handcuff. The suspect suddenly pulled a gun out of his pants pocket and shot Meyers in his abdomen. Officer James jumped onto the suspect, and the three men went to the ground. Not wanting to accidentally shoot his fellow officer, Meyers struck the man with his gun. The suspect fired twice more, wounding James and fatally striking Meyers in the chest. He then ran away, with James firing at him.

"The suspect was cornered in a house about three blocks away, where he committed suicide. It was discovered later that he had been wanted on a murder charge out of California."

Nick Meyers's murder was brutal for everyone. In those days, citizens supported the police, and the outpouring of sympathy for the victims was overwhelming. Dale took it especially hard because he and Nick had formed a tight bond that extended to off the job.

Nick's wife asked Dale and me to be pallbearers, an honor I wasn't expecting. I sat a few chairs away from her at the graveside. I will never forget the look of profound grief on her face as she extended her hands to accept the folded American flag. They had three children and expecting a fourth at the time of her husband's murder.

Dale was of tremendous help with Nick's wife over the weeks that followed.

A WORD ABOUT STREET GANGS

I worked in the PD's Gang Enforcement Unit for four years as an intelligence officer for white supremacy gangs. When violence surged among other groups—black, Hispanic, Southeast Asian, and white gangs unrelated to skinheads—I helped the unit's street enforcement teams.

In the latter 1980s and into the 1990s, street gangs were deadly and an ongoing threat to the communities as they wantonly sprayed bullets into crowds, parties, cars, parks, and even funerals. Gunfire was a threat virtually every night in some neighborhoods. It was so prevalent that many families routinely hid in the deep recesses of their homes to hide from stray rounds. One elderly man told me that he and his wife frequently took cover in their bathtub when neighborhood gangs fought.

One night I was asked to assist patrolling with the enforcement officers because the war between Bloods and Crips had intensified. The night before, one of the gangs drove down an alley, spotted their target house, and sprayed it with rounds. One bullet passed through the outer wall of a baby's room and struck and killed a sleeping infant. Every officer in the unit volunteered to find the shooter.

When three skinheads beat an Ethiopian man to death with a baseball bat, the story made international news, bringing attention and more skinheads to our city. As a result, the surge in white supremacist violence was unprecedented in the country.

Hispanic gangs mostly killed each other, as did Asian gangbangers. Their gunfire, often undisciplined spraying, was at times a nightly occurrence.

Today, members no longer wear specific clothing depicting which gang they belonged to, but they haven't gone away, and the killing continues.

CHAPTER 7

A Dead Gangbanger

One day, my sergeant came to my desk and told my partner and me to head up to a small town 90 minutes east of Portland to assist the police department there. An officer had shot and killed a man they suspected was a gang member from our city. We were happy to do it because the drive up the Columbia River Gorge would be a pleasant escape.

We met with officers at the city morgue's front office. We were told that an officer responded to a break-in in progress at a local gun store the night before. He confronted the burglar as he climbed out the broken front plate-glass window, his arms loaded with an assortment of rifles.

The suspect dropped all but one. He pointed it at the officer who quickly fired his own weapon, the round penetrating the suspect's heart. Nonetheless—and this isn't unusual—the thief ran over 100 feet before he fell dead.

The officers wanted us to look at the dead man's tattoos and clothing to see if we thought he was one of our gangbangers. We followed them and the medical examiner into the cooler.

The deceased was stretched out naked on a gurney. The hole over his heart had been wiped clean. He had gang affiliate tattoos on his arms and chest that tied him into a black gang. My partner and I didn't usually work Bloods and Crips, so we didn't know him. We needed to take photos to show the gangs' intelligence officer back in Portland.

I began snapping pics with a Polaroid. The gurney was about waist-high, but with the deceased lying on it, front side up, he was near my solar plexus level. With today's cell phones, I could have simply reached over and captured a straight-on face pic. But not with a Polaroid.

So I slid a chair up to him, set one foot on the seat and my other on the gurney on the other side of his torso. I bent down within a couple of feet from his face and took several photos. I was hoping the chair would stay put and that my foot next to the body wouldn't slip, the result of which would be me getting much closer than I wanted.

I got the pics, and we headed back to Portland.

————————————

The young man made a series of bad choices that night. 1) He didn't seem to consider that a gun store would have an alarm system. 2) He determined that smashing out a 6'x6' front plate window was the best way to make entry. 3) He greedily took an arm full of rifles that are hard to carry even when not struggling to escape through a jaggedly broken window. 4) When the police confronted him, he dropped all but one and pointed the empty weapon at them. 5) He didn't take a single round of ammunition with him.

There are many famous quotes about poor decision-making, such as, "Good decisions come from experience. Experience comes from making bad decisions." Yes, we learn from our bad choices. Some people make repeated bad decisions before the learning part finally kicks in.

The gun thief, who turned out to be a known gangbanger in Portland, had a history of making bad choices, many that hurt innocent people. His last one—pointing an empty rifle at a police officer—was so grievous and downright foolish that it ended any possibility of his learning.

It also stopped him from making more victims.

CHAPTER 8

Two Gangbangers' Funerals

It was common for gangs in Portland to threaten to do drive-by shootings at a rival gang member's funeral. There had been retaliatory drive-bys in Los Angeles during gang member funerals, so we always took such threats seriously. Sometimes we stationed gang enforcement officers in front of the funeral home to serve as a presence. Other times, they parked on side streets that offered a clear view of the outside proceedings. When a rival gang car was spotted, it was stopped.

When the word on the street was considered good (as opposed to rumor) that a drive-by was planned, everyone in the gang unit worked the threat.

There were times we had to guard the body during open-casket viewing. It was typical for the deceased (all of them shooting victims) to be dressed in full gang attire, distinctive colors to designate their affiliation. Viewers of the deceased lined up wearing gang colors and would flash hand signs as they passed the body. Even sadder were mothers who brought their young children to the funeral wearing colors. This included babies.

Here are two instances in which I was assigned to guard gang members' bodies as they lay in funeral homes.

A Southeast Asian Gang Member

As I've mentioned, though I worked white supremacy crimes, I often helped the other gang intelligence officers. This time, I assisted the Southeast Asian intelligence officer guard a gang member lying in an open gasket. The young man had been shot in the forehead. Since the family wanted the deceased to wear the gang's trademark do-rag, the mortician used it to cover the bullet hole.

Joss paper (fake money) was stacked on the floor around the coffin, as well as baskets of fruit. Loose joss had also been placed inside the coffin on and around the body. Incense sticks burned here and there. Mourners came and went throughout the day, bowing, leaving joss and fruit, and eyeing my partner and me. No doubt older people wondered why serious-looking Caucasian men were closely watching the goings-on; the younger ones knew why. Some gang members recognized my partner since he had talked to them in the past. They would do a quick bow to the coffin and hurry out the door.

A couple of hours into the showing, and thankfully when there wasn't anyone viewing the body, we noticed the hole in the dead man's head was leaking grey gunk. Whatever it was streamed out from under the do-rag and ran down his cheek. I went to the front office and told the secretary what was happening. Within minutes, one of the funeral people was on the scene and matter-of-factly plugged the wound.

Shortly afterward, new people arrived to give their respects, which went without further incident.

I couldn't help but wonder what the older Vietnamese thought as they passed by the coffin to view the dead gangbanger dressed in his regalia. Fifteen years earlier, there had been a massive influx of Vietnamese into Portland, most of them moving into a sprawling apartment complex soon nicknamed "Little Saigon." The deceased had to have been just a toddler when his family settled in Portland.

Some who came to this country were wealthy and made their way across the sea in airplanes. The poorer crossed the dangerous ocean in overcrowded, rickety boats. There is no record of how many died from illness during the crossing or went down in leaking boats. Many of the parents of small ones or soon-to-be parents didn't speak a word of English.

Their children were sent to American schools unprepared, with teachers who didn't speak the language. The Vietnamese kids were viewed by others their age as different and talked "funny." Those Vietnamese kids who did know some English, spoke it poorly. Very quickly, the Vietnamese kids became the target of bullying.

In self-defense, the Vietnamese kids joined forces for strength in numbers. Over time, some groups evolved into criminal gangs that committed extortion, robbery, assaults, and murder. Interestingly, during the time I worked in the Gang Unit, all the murders of Southeast Asians were perpetrated by other Southeast Asians. That wasn't the case in other jurisdictions.

When the older generation saw their children lying in coffins, did they wonder if it would have been better to have stayed in South Vietnam under North Vietnam's rule? Did the older people blame themselves for what had become of some of their children?

As a Vietnam veteran, I was shocked when Vietnamese refugees began coming into my city. When I flew out of the country and looked out the window at the ground pitted with bomb craters, I remember thinking, I'll never see this godforsaken place and the people again. Little did I know that there would be a massive influx of Vietnamese into my hometown five years later.

I would subsequently have Vietnamese friends and martial arts students. Several were of great help when I worked on two books about Vietnam.

The young man in the coffin with the leaking bullet hole in his head was the only dead Southeast Asian gangbanger I saw during my time in the unit. There were others, but I wasn't involved in those cases.

A Black Gang Member

On another occasion, I was asked to help the black gang intelligence officer stand guard at the viewing of a deceased young man who had fallen by rival gang gunfire. There was good intel that the rival gang might come and disrupt things as people came to show their respects.

The coffin, the lid closed, rested on a table surrounded by flowers. We stood in the lobby with the deceased, where we had a visual of the parking lot and the cemetery off to the right. We stood there for a while, and when no one showed up, we sat down facing the parking lot. The other intel officer filled me in on the shooting that took the man's life. It was a classic gangbanger homicide, a revenge shooting because the gunman had determined or imagined that he had been disrespected somehow.

The only person who showed up to look at the closed coffin, I knew by reputation.

His street name was Huge Man, which wasn't all that creative considering he was 6'5", 325 pounds. My first thought when I saw him out in the parking lot wrestling himself out from behind his steering wheel was that should we have to arrest him, and he resisted, the ensuing fight would probably level the funeral parlor. While Huge Man stood on the other side of his car for a long moment scanning the street out front, my partner called Records Division for a quick warrant check. He was clear, no warrants. The funeral parlor would remain unbroken.

Huge Man walked around to the back of his car, exposing all of his big self to us, though he couldn't see my partner and me because the lobby doors were tinted. Our unmarked vehicles, though they never fooled anyone, were parked out of sight. He stood gang-style behind his car, one foot pointing straight ahead, the heel of his other against the inside of the first foot, to form a T. It was silly looking. Still, it was an engrained gang pose, as was how he held his head: his chin high, his eyes forward.

Huge Man wore an oversized 49s sports jacket; I couldn't imagine how a 325-pound man found one that was *too* large. His trousers hung below his butt, the pant legs bunched around the tops of his expensive running shoes. He held the pose for several seconds and then lumbered toward the lobby, one hand holding up his pants.

He pulled open the doors, his eyes widening comically at the sight of two gang cops standing by the coffin. My partner greeted him, and the banger gave him a short nod. Huge Man moved over to the coffin and looked at it for a long moment. Was he thinking they would need an extra-large one for him? If he was, it was prophetic because he didn't have long to live.

Huge Man exchanged a few words with my partner, then left, crossing the lot back to his car. He again stood there as if posing for a photo that depicted the gang stance and attire. He finally left without incident.

Not long after, Huge Man was sitting in a house with other bangers watching television. What happened next is unclear because not a single person would cooperate with detectives. I spoke with one of the homicide detectives while writing this book, and he said the case went unsolved. This was no fault of his as he was an excellent investigator. But no one would talk to him, period, since everyone on both sides hated Huge Man. At one point during the investigation, the detective said, "I think I'm the only one who cares who killed the guy." The street officers talked with all their contacts, and not one was forthcoming. There were a couple of versions floating around, but no names attached to them.

One was that some of Huge Man's buddies said they were going out for a beer run and would be back. Huge Man shrugged his indifference and continued to watch the tube. As soon as the other bangers were outside, they stepped over to the living room window and fired through the glass, killing Huge Man, a member of their own gang.

The other version is that a rival gang shot him, the rounds punching through the plate glass window, the same way mobster Bugsy Siegel was killed in 1947.

My takeaway on the funeral home contact with Huge Man was that he was performing for himself. He couldn't see into the lobby, and our unmarked police cars were nowhere in view. His was the only car in the large lot, and he parked far enough away from the street that it would be difficult for passing cars to see him.

Nonetheless, he went through all the gang schtick when he got out of his ride. He wore his blatant gang attire, he stood with one foot perpendicular to the other, and his chin lifted as though looking at a distant airplane. Then he strutted badass across the parking lot to the entrance doors.

But for whom was his performance? As far as he could see, there wasn't a soul watching him. Still, to use today's expression, he was workin' it. Not for an audience but for himself. This was because his self-image, so deeply entrenched in his mind, was that he was a gangbanger 24/7 even when he was by himself.

As I pointed out in my presentations to the community, this mindset should be considered especially concerning. This man, and thousands like him in the white supremacy, Hispanic, Asian, and white gangs, lived and breathed—their gang. It was who they were right down to their cells, and it was who they would die for—and kill for.

A WORD ABOUT OTHER KILLING WEAPONS

Shooting someone is clean unless it's done at close range, in which case the shooter gets blowback blood splatter all over them.

Stabbing with a knife, a glass shard, or a screwdriver can be clean if it's done to a fatal target and the blade is left in the body. However, it gets sloppy when the victim is stabbed and sliced multiple times, especially to arteries.

Kicking someone with shoes or heavy boots increases the potential for a fatality. When I worked skinheads in the Gang Enforcement Team, I had a case in which a white supremacist "curb-stomped" a man. This is a technique taken from Nazi Germany when a Gestapo would order a prisoner to lie down in the gutter and place his open mouth over the edge of a curb. Since the Gestapo wore relatively light footwear, they would order a German infantry soldier to stomp the back of the victim's head with their heavier boots. The technique would break the victim's jaw and knock out several teeth. Sometimes it caused death from a broken neck.

The skinhead in my case succeeded in severely injuring the man; he might have killed him if passersby hadn't intervened.

Assaulting someone with environmental weapons increases the risk of death. I investigated a few that could have caused a fatality if others present hadn't stopped the assault.

Here are four off the top of my head.

⬧ Two roommates fought, one man beating the other with a VCR. A friend stopped the assailant just in time.

⬧ A one-legged man removed his artificial leg and used it to beat a man severely before he was stopped.

✧ An assailant placed an injured man's head on the edge of a dumpster and repeatedly slammed the large metal lid down on the back of his skull. My partner and I stopped him short of killing the man.

✧ A transient couple were sleeping in a sleeping bag in a park on the edge of skid row. The man woke up in the middle of the night to the sounds of his girlfriend having sex in a nearby sleeping bag. In a rage, he bought a can of gasoline from a nearby service station, brought it back to the campsite, and poured it over the sleeping bag containing his girlfriend and her new lover, their heads covered. My partner and I caught him just as he was preparing to light a match. When the commotion awakened the couple in the bag, the woman turned out not to be the man's girlfriend. In fact, it was a different sleeping bag. His girlfriend and her new friend left while he was buying the gasoline, and a new couple with a similar sleeping bag took their place. They were understandably upset when they realized how close they came to being set ablaze.

Here are a few cases where people used a baseball bat, their bare hands, and an automobile to take a life.

CHAPTER 9

A Hate Crime Murder

A hate crime is perpetrated against an individual or group with specific characteristics defined by law. Specifically, hate crime laws are crimes committed because of the victim's(s') perceived or actual race, color, religion, national origin, sexual orientation, gender, age, gender identity, or disability.

Hate crimes are usually violent—assault, murder, arson, vandalism, or threats to commit such crimes. In some cases, it includes conspiring or asking another person to commit such crimes, even if the crime was never carried out.

Hate crimes were established because they have a broader effect than most other kinds. An assault or murder based on the victim's sexual orientation, race, gender, and so on affects the target and others like them, including entire communities.

I worked in the Portland Police Bureau's Gang Enforcement Team's White Supremacy Unit for a few years at the peak of the racist skinhead movement. (Note: Some skinheads were anti-racism. For ease of writing, from this point on, when referencing "skins" or "skinheads," I'm referring to the racist type.) The skins targeted blacks, Asians, gays, and anyone else they thought different. As a result, other people like the targeted victims lived in fear for themselves, their families, and friends.

In 1988, skinhead crimes based on hate of certain groups sprang up seemingly overnight. (Hate Crime law didn't exist at the time). As the Crime Analyst at Central Precinct, I began compiling reports of racist crimes while simultaneously learning what skinheads were about with their shaved heads, flight jackets, Nazi tattoos, Doc Marten boots, and dangling suspenders. When one skinhead stabbed a guy in a nightclub then licked the blade off in front of the crowd, I knew they were going to be a problem.

The wave of racist motivated crimes continued through 1988. Then on November 12, Portland was about to get infamous.

9-1-1 operator: *"Police radio. What is your emergency?"*
Female caller: "We need the police to Thirty-First and Southeast Pine Street. I just heard gunshots."

But they weren't gunshots at all. They were the sounds of a Louisville Slugger cracking a human head. (A Louisville Slugger is a finely crafted baseball bat for swing precision and power, according to the company.) The target that chilly night was not a baseball, but a dark-skinned human being, what the murdering skinheads referred to as "mud people."

Mulugeta Seraw, 28, moved to Portland, Oregon, to further his education by obtaining a degree in business from Portland Community College while working multiple jobs to provide for his wife and six-year-old son still in Ethiopia. Instead, he was beaten to death by three members of a neo-Nazi gang calling themselves East Side White Pride, part of a larger organization, White Aryan Resistance (WAR).

Late in the evening, skinheads Kyle Brewster, Kenneth Murray "Ken Death" Mieske, and Steve Strasser pulled up behind a car in the middle of the street. Two Ethiopian men were inside; a third, Seraw, had just gotten out to go into his apartment. At first, the three skinheads cursed the Ethiopians out their car windows. Then they got out and began to assault them with their steel-toed boots. At one point, Mieske came up behind Seraw and struck him twice on the head with the Louisville Slugger bat.

As Seraw lay bleeding on the pavement, Mieske struck one more time. The final blow "crushed his head between the bat and the hard pavement," said one of the investigating detectives. (Because his head was supported by the pavement, the energy from the bat was 100 percent absorbed into the skull.)

One week later, Brewster, Mieske, and Strasser were arrested by our detectives and subsequently convicted. Mieske pleaded guilty to first-degree murder and was sentenced to life imprisonment. Brewster and Strasser pleaded guilty to assault and manslaughter charges and were given 20-year sentences.

In an unprecedented civil trial, the Southern Poverty Law Center employed an innovative legal strategy to hold Metzger and WAR liable for the wrongful death of Mulugeta Seraw. The Center won a $12.5 million verdict that effectively put the racist hate group and their many minor-league gangs out of business. The verdict awarded the proceeds to Mulugeta's family.

Media came from all over the globe to cover the tense proceedings. Because of white supremacists' continual threats against the city, the PD positioned sniper teams on rooftops and a surveillance helicopter to hover above the streets. The bomb squad was on standby in response to numerous threats, and dozens of uniformed police officers formed a ring around the courthouse each morning.

The PD had to protect Tom Metzger and his seven skinhead goons. I was put in charge of a four-person protection detail. We picked up Metzger and his people every day during the two-week trial and drove them in a large van with a follow car to the courthouse. When we got the green light from a sergeant by radio, we roared up to the drop point, guarded by SWAT officers. We slid open the van's side door, scurried Metzger, who was wearing a bulletproof vest, and the goons, not provided vests, down an opening in the sidewalk. From there, we moved along an underground passageway to an elevator and zipped up to the fifth floor. We stood by in an empty room until we were told to bring the hate group into the courtroom.

Even with the massive security, our van was fired on by someone with bow and arrows. (Someone who apparently thought Oregon was still the wild west.) It was assumed the shooter was positioned on a rooftop out of sight of our snipers.

My roughly four years submerged in the world of white supremacists and the hate they wallowed in was one of the strangest periods of my police career. The press made me an expert in white supremacy before I knew anything about it, thus forcing me to read and study everything I could on the subject.

Because I was in the news all the time, the skinheads made me "the face" of the Portland Police Bureau. In reality, I was just a guy standing in the wrong place at the wrong time when all of it exploded.

This made me a target during the skinheads' protests, their acts of vandalism, and their chanting. On one occasion, they draped a white Ku Klux Klan-type sheet over a 25-foot-high statue of Joan of Arc on a horse in the center of a traffic circle. Then they hung a large sign over her neck that read, "Officer Christensen." They also put me at the top of a hit list to kill.

I was glad when things finally died down enough to leave the unit and go back to Central Precinct for my last years on the PD.

Sadly, white supremacy hasn't gone away. As I write this, we're seeing hate groups again in the news.

CHAPTER 10

Shaken Baby Murder

For almost seven years, I edited the Portland Police monthly newspaper, *The Rap Sheet*. I wrote a column and did features on officers, various units, new laws, crazy crooks, and legal developments. One day, I went to the morgue to write a story about medical examiners and their work. I had been retired for a couple of years, but most examiners knew me from working with them on many occasions.

One led me around the place, pointing out what they did when a deceased person was admitted into the system. Every time I had been to the cooler, there were always bodies on gurneys awaiting their turn for processing. This time the place was packed with the deceased, most of whom looked under 30 years. I asked why.

"Some bad drugs came into Portland," the ME said.

I don't remember what drug it was, but I'm guessing it was some form of heroin, an opioid that had been the cause of several upticks in drug-related deaths in the past. This is discussed elsewhere in this book.

While some of the bodies were still clothed, all were barefoot with ID tags looped around their big toes. Across from them and against a wall, a wooden stand with multiple shelves held their shoes, two dozen of them, an indicator of how bad the dope was. I snapped a photo of it for the article.

After getting enough info and pics for my story, we went back into the office area, where we caught up with each other's lives. At one point, a medical examiner came in who had been out on a call. He was carrying a small blanket-wrapped bundle. He set it down and greeted me. We exchanged pleasantries then I asked what he had.

"Shaken baby syndrome," he said softly. "The baby was probably keeping the mother up at night, or maybe it was some other reason. She shook him so hard it killed him."

"Did the police arrest her?"

"Oh yeah, and they had a hell of a fight. She wouldn't let go of the baby." He unwrapped the blanket enough to expose the infant's face, shoulders, and a little of the chest. There were bruises on all visible surfaces. "The mother, or someone else, did other things to the child too."

Unaware I had been holding my breath, I exhaled and stepped away from the bundle. "I hope there's a special place in Hell for who did it," I managed.

The ME nodded, gently rewrapped the bundle, and headed toward the cooler.

I investigated child abuse cases when I worked in the Juvenile Division. While it had its horrific moments, I got great satisfaction hauling some cowardly swine to jail. It was also satisfying to know they would be in prison with inmates who looked down on child abusers and would give the cowards lots of unwanted attention.

"Man's inhumanity to man makes countless thousands mourn," wrote poet Robert Burns in 1785 in his poem, "Man was made to mourn." If I may add, never more so than when it comes to victimized children.

I discovered while working abuse cases that some were unadulterated brutality, others were the result of a lack of education as to how to parent, from babyhood all the way into the terrible teens. Oh, they knew how to make a baby, though too often it wasn't their intention. But they hadn't a clue how to be a parent.

I believe shaken baby syndrome and other forms of abuse were sometimes due to parents not establishing a sleeping and eating schedule for their infants. That lack of knowledge created hungry and tired babies that showed their discomfort by constant crying. When we saw this was the case, we set the parents up for classes.

Regarding shaken baby syndrome, the interested reader can check out mayoclinic.org, then search "shaken baby syndrome."

Law enforcement should take special note of this since the shaken baby syndrome is often misdiagnosed. Knowledge is power.

CHAPTER 11

Attempted Murder And A Self-Defense Death

This occurred in my town just a few years ago and made news across the country. At the time, I was working on a book titled *Self-Defense for Women: Fight Back.* Because the case involved a nurse who fought her assailant, I tracked her down, and we had a chat. Here is a short version of what happened.

One night, the 51-year-old nurse returned home after a long shift working in the ER at one of Portland's hospitals. She had barely stepped through the door when an intruder, armed with a claw hammer, charged at her from a side room and smashed it into her head. Incredibly, the nurse didn't lose consciousness and began fighting the man who it would turn out was hired by her husband to kill her.

They struggled in a ferocious battle all over the room, punching and kicking each other. At one point, the nurse managed to rip the hammer from the assailant's hand and commenced beating his body as he simultaneously and ferociously chewed on her flesh like a beast gone mad.

The nurse outweighed her assailant by 80 pounds and had years of experience battling violent patients in the ER. She managed to fight her way behind him and wrap her arm around his neck. He fought desperately against her deadly hold. Still, she continued to constrict his breath from his lungs and vital oxygen to his brain.

With each passing second, the hired killer grew weaker and weaker until his brain slipped into unconsciousness, and his heart finally ceased to beat.

Death by strangulation, the autopsy report said.

Her husband was subsequently sentenced to 10 years for his role in the attempted murder.

I hope this woman has come to terms with what she had to do.

I've written much about the psychological effects of using deadly force. About a third of the people are affected for a long while after, sometimes their entire lives. I've worked with officers and have known war veterans who were terribly traumatized from taking a life no matter how justified the situation.

I've also known people who were able to come to terms with it and have gone on to live happy and productive lives.

So often on the job, I had homeowners, men mostly, tell me with a chest inflated with bravado how they would "blow away" a burglar in their home. This was despite our district attorney at the time telling Portlanders that he would prosecute anyone who did that. "A thief stealing your TV is not an excuse to kill him," the DA said.

When I told homeowners this, most said they didn't care. "Someone breaks into my home," they'd snarl, their faces red, "I'll shoot them dead where they stand."

"Well, sir," I'd say, "you just made two mistakes. You just told a cop you will kill a burglar, and I'll have to testify in court should you do it. Second, you must deal with the aftermath, the public condemnation, the liberal press, attorney fees, lawsuits, and the possibility of imprisonment. Plus, you will have to live here knowing that that place right there on the floor is where a man died by your hand."

I never told them that I understood and sympathized with their determination to protect their home. My intent was to get them to see beyond their blind intention to take a life and understand the complicated consequences of their actions.

CHAPTER 12

Dead Woman Under Car

It was a cold, damp Sunday morning, the fog reducing visibility to half a block. I was riding passenger as my partner, Tom, talked about his kitchen remodeling. The left side of the street was lined with dilapidated pre-World War II houses. There was a large field of yellowed dead weeds on the right side and a few cars parked along the curb. As we were about even with a black sedan, my eye alerted on a clump of something underneath it.

There was lots of garbage strewn along the gutters and under cars, but whatever was under the sedan didn't look right.

"Hold on, Tom," I said. "Something's under that Ford."

"Garbage?"

"Probably, but maybe a person."

He backed us until we were a car length behind the one in question.

"Still not sure," I said, getting out. "Let's check,"

We didn't see the tangled body parts and a severely mangled female face until we got down on our knees and looked under the rear bumper.

"I think she's caught," I said, crawling under the car to look closer. "She is. She's completed tangled in the undercarriage." We asked dispatch for a sergeant to come to the scene and ordered a tow truck to lift the vehicle's back end.

While we waited, we noted the minor damage on the vehicle's front and ran a registration on the license plate. We scanned the street and the field next to it for evidence of the impact. Nothing. I walked about 40 yards to the intersection to see if there was anything there.

I found a smear of blood a few feet short of where the car would have made the turn. A quarter of a block farther, I found another swath of the blood, this one with broken teeth and strands of dark hair in it. Unless the victim had been killed instantly, she must have screamed, which meant the driver had to have known she was under the vehicle. There was more evidence farther down the street and more on a cross street a block away.

A tow truck arrived just as I got back to the scene. A dozen people had gathered, braving the morning chill. Three TV news crews were setting up, all on the street side of the car. The tow truck proved too small for the task, so we ordered a larger one, which took another half hour to arrive.

When the monster tow truck rumbled in, the rubberneckers had increased to 50 people. The medical examiner was on site, ready to collect the remains, and our Criminalistics crew was on standby to process the scene. Tom and I stood on the edge of the field; everyone else had gathered in the street on the other side of the car. The tow truck driver was clearly bothered by crawling under the car's back end to attach the hooks close to a mutilated body.

As TV cameras rolled, the tow truck began to lift the car's back end higher and higher. Just then, the harsh winter sun lasered through the clouds, hitting my sensitive eyes. I squinted and grimaced with most of my teeth just as the body dropped away from the undercarriage.

Most of it, anyway. A broken and twisted leg remained caught, leaving the poor woman hanging upside down, swaying in the air.

The crowd gasped and quickly turned away, except those who enjoyed seeing such a thing. There are always those.

TV media broadcasted the story on the 5 o'clock news. They blurred the body but left Tom and me in high definition. My toothy grimace from the sudden sunburst made it look as if I were laughing.

I heard about it the next day from the command staff, which meant I had to explain myself repeatedly.

The subsequent investigation by our detectives disclosed the death was a homicide, the result of an argument in the driveway of a bar a few blocks away. The male had deliberately run the female down and dragged her to where we found the body later.

Finding a mangled body under a car was one way to wake up on a dreary Sunday morning just after leaving the precinct. Still, it was better we found it than neighborhood children. Coincidentally, we found the woman four blocks from the morgue.

Five years earlier, I was working with a coach in Traffic Division when dispatch notified all cars that a dump truck loaded with gravel had run over a child. With a vehicle that heavy carrying a full load of gravel to boot, the driver had no idea what had happened and that the child was still tangled underneath his rig. All available cars began looking for the truck. My coach and I cruised all the streets near a sand and gravel company, stopping a few, explaining to the drivers what we were doing, then checking under their rigs.

An hour later, another police unit located the right truck. We heard that the driver was inconsolable with grief, as were the parents. As always, the officers involved had to deal with it in their own way.

Some officers tried to blot out haunted sights, smells, and sounds with alcohol. Others sought comfort in their families, church, coaching sports, or participating in athletics.

Still, no matter how the officer tried, some images remain.

A WORD ABOUT PROSTITUTES

I have always been fascinated with what I call subcultures; I've written on several, including a book titled *Hookers, Tricks, and Cops*. It's a world unfamiliar to most, but it's one that people are curious about, though they pretend not to be.

I was fascinated with this subculture as a rookie, and I took advantage of every contact to learn more about it. I wanted to know who the hookers and customers were. Why they were pedaling their bodies on the street. Why they were driving around neighborhoods looking for sex from strangers. Did they have families? Wives? Husbands? Kids? Parents?

It didn't take long, though, before I grew weary of it and saw it for what it was: ugly, sordid, degrading, violent, poignant, and immensely sad.

I saw 19- and 20-year-old women who looked 40 after two years selling themselves from street corners—tired, worn, defeated, and numb to everything. I saw fresh-faced teens who hadn't a clue what they were getting themselves into, though they would have a good idea within a week or two. The youngest I knew of was 13 years old, the daughter of a local celebrity. The oldest was a toothless woman in her 60s, her face and body far older than her years. She did a brisk business, though. So, did her daughter, who often worked with her.

Some tricks got their kicks using the girls as punching bags. Hookers who had strolled the streets for a few months displayed black eyes, broken teeth, and bruised arms. The especially sadistic men liked to do more than *just* beat them.

Prostitutes could be violent too. Some would bring a trick to a hotel room where one or two other girls waited in closets to spring out to assault and rob. Sometimes it was the hooker's boyfriend who assaulted and robbed the customer. We knew it happened, but few men dared to file a complaint with the police.

Pimps often beat the girls when they didn't earn enough money, kept more than their allotted share, or were so sopped with drugs they couldn't work. Ironically, pimps beat tricks when they were caught harming the girls.

The customers were often products of bad marriages or sick minds. Instead of seeking help for their issues, they chose to steer their cars to the curb and enter the seedy and dangerous world of pandering and flesh peddling.

CHAPTER 13

The Day Kandy Saw Her Future

I saw Kandy at least three or four times a week as she promenaded on a busy boulevard densely populated with other hookers. She was about 30 years old, emaciated, with pale skin and sunken cheeks. She told us that she was frequently sick and that she had had both breasts removed two years earlier because of cancer. Dan and I liked her, finding her personable, funny, and articulate.

The day we met Kandy, we had been cruising along the street when we spotted a woman struggling to get away from a slick-looking guy in a full-length fur coat. We leaped out just as the screaming, kicking, and flailing progressed into the middle of the busy street. We saved both from getting run over, arrested the pimp, and became forever in Kandy's debt.

Whenever we saw her working her corner, we always pulled over to ask how she was doing. She often told us of tricks flashing far too much money for their station in life or about guys bragging about robbing a 7-Eleven or doing a bank job. She got good at getting descriptions of the guys, and sometimes she got their license plate numbers.

I'm sure she knew lots of other crooks, too, but she told us only about those she didn't like.

The decaying Four Winds Motel sat in a weed-choked lot three blocks off the main street of our beat. I couldn't imagine any straight citizen staying there unless they enjoyed filth, rats, and cockroaches. The owner didn't need them anyway since the hookers and tricks kept the place solvent. The customer had to pay for the room as well as the hooker's treats.

One driveway led into the parking area of the horseshoe-shaped structure, and another at the other end of the lot led out into a rundown, residential neighborhood. In a typical shift, Dan and I cruised the lot at least once, sometimes three or four times when there were lots of hookers on the street. This kept our presence visible so that the tricks would behave themselves, and the hookers would think twice before they robbed one.

The reader might wonder why we, regular patrol officers, didn't arrest them for prostitution. In my state, the police need three elements to arrest a prostitute: the cost, the act, and an admission by the hooker. They aren't likely to give uniform officers this information. So every so often, the precinct would conduct undercover prostitution stings. Female officers would pose as street hookers, or male officers would wear civilian clothes and pose as tricks. A real customer could be arrested when he told an undercover female officer what he wanted and what he would pay. The real female hooker could be charged when she told the undercover male officer what sex act she would do and for how much.

One day we were cruising through the lot when Kandy burst from the door of one of the rooms. "Christensen! Christensen!" She was clutching her unbuttoned blouse, crying, hyperventilating, and continually looking back toward the motel door.

I anchored the car. "What's the matter?"

"The son-of-a-bitch is still inside the room," she sobbed. "Go in there and kick his ass, will you?"

Dan opened the back door of the police car and motioned for her to have a seat. "Tell us what happened," he said. She half fell onto the backseat, bunching her blouse together with her right hand while favoring her left. That's when I noticed the charred black and red circles in the finger webs of her left hand.

I pointed at her wrist. "What …?"

"The bastard burned me with his cigarette," she grimaced. "He pinned me to the bed and stuck his cigarette between my fingers. He's a sick mother-fucker."

We arrested the guy without incident, which is usually the case with men who like to abuse women; they don't like to fight male cops.

Kandy didn't follow through with the district attorney, shrugging her shoulders when we asked her why a few days later. "Comes with the territory," she said with a wave of her scarred hand.

A month or two later, dispatch sent Dan and me to the medical examiner's office located in our beat. It was another occasion when they wanted to see if we could identify a body found in the neighborhood.

"Someone found her behind a house on 9th and Morris," the medical examiner said as a way of greeting when we came into the front office. "The lady was wearing cutoff jeans, red halter top, blond wig, and high heels." We followed him through a heavy steel door, through another set of heavy doors, and into a mostly chrome room where three bodies lay neatly on gurneys. One of them was a naked woman staring lifelessly into the harsh, white light hanging over her head. The ME stopped at her gurney. "She had half a dozen condoms in her pocket, no identification, so we thought she might be one of your ladies of the evening."

I glanced over at two elderly naked men lying quietly on the other two gurneys. When I looked back, the ME was pulling the woman's chin toward us. "Know her?" he asked.

Dan and I shook our heads. "I've seen her around," my partner said, "but I can't remember her name." I concurred.

The M.E. sighed. "We'll Jane Doe her then."

"How about if we bring in a working lady to look at her?" I asked.

"Sure. It would save me a lot of work."

Two hours later, we spotted Kandy working her usual corner. We asked if she would help us identify someone in the morgue.

"How did she die?" she asked hesitantly.

"Shot in the chest," Dan said, "but you don't have to look at the injury. Just her face. A sheet covers the rest of her."

It was obvious Kandy didn't want to do it, but she reluctantly agreed to help since she liked us. I noticed a tad of morbid curiosity, too.

When I introduced the M.E. to Kandy, I was amused to see his eyes roam her emaciated body with the curiosity of a man, not a doctor. "Thanks for helping us," he said. "She's in the back here."

She moved on eggshells toward the sheet-covered gurney, her hands trembling and her eyes staring trance-like at the white covering. To my surprise and Kandy's shock, the M. E. pulled the sheet completely off the naked body. Her eyes widened at the ugly bullet hole, then moved up to the woman's dead face.

"Oh God!" she screamed, covering her mouth with her hands. "Oh God, oh God!" Then shouted at Dan and me, "You bastards! You bastards," and spun and bolted from the room.

"Hmm, that went well," Dan mused as we started after her.

"She went that-a-way," a secretary in the outer office told us, pointing toward the open front door.

We didn't see her for two days. When we pulled to the curb on the third, she was madder than a wet hornet.

"You guys are assholes," she said accusingly, her eyes tearing. "Making me look at Brenda like that. You said I wouldn't see the bullet—"

"Brenda," Dan said, snapping his fingers. "That's it, Brenda Luke."

There was no calming Kandy that day or, for that matter, the following several times we tried to talk to her. I think when she came face to face with a dead coworker, she got slapped with her own mortality and the harsh reality as to what can happen in her line of work.

Soon after, I left that district for another job on the police bureau. I saw Kandy downtown about 10 years later, and she looked even skinnier, paler, and sicklier. In fact, she was so emaciated that she looked terminal. Given her line of work, she no doubt had a long grocery list of diseases.

I doubt she is still alive.

CHAPTER 14

The Hooker And The Tow Truck Driver

The medical examiner held the woman's breasts in his hands.

The doc had sliced a large square of flesh around them, removed the section from the woman's chest, and was holding it in his gloved palms when Dan and I walked into the autopsy room.

"What do you think?" he asked casually and without humor, though there wasn't anything funny about it, anyway. Still, it was strange to see him standing there, looking like a waiter with a tray.

"I mean the puncture marks." He held the breasts closer for us to examine.

My stomach flip-flopped. "Four holes," I managed.

He rotated the square section of flesh. "Actually, there are five. See here? Four that form a square and one in the middle, like the five-die in a game of dice."

Dan and I had been called to the morgue to see if we could identify the woman. We worked an area thick with druggies and hookers, folks who too often concluded their day on a metal slab. As the M.E. spoke, I noticed a pair of silver satin shorts and white boots under her gurney.

"There are bruises on the neck," he noted, pointing at the blond woman with his free hand. Her frozen mouth yawned in an ugly grimace, and her partially closed, lifeless eyes seemed to freeze-frame some sort of horror. "Choke marks. My guess is that the killer held his arm around her neck from behind." The M.E pantomimed the action in the air. "And then used his other hand to reach around and stab her repeatedly above her breasts."

"Any idea what he used?" Dan asked.

"I'm thinking a Philip's screwdriver," the M.E. said, setting the square of breasts down in the woman's chest cavity, but upside down. "See the little cross cuts in the punctures? A Philip's screwdriver makes those."

"Where was she found?" Dan asked.

"Night officers called us at one a.m. A late-night jogger found her sprawled alongside the road on South Standard in an illegal dumpsite. Right now, I'm thinking she was killed a little earlier in the evening."

We couldn't identify the woman. Maybe she was new in town, or perhaps she strolled at night after we ended our shift. Some hookers worked only during the day, and others worked in the evenings, shift work.

A couple of days later, one of the investigating detectives stopped us in East Precinct and said he had information the suspect might be a mechanic or a tow truck driver.

"Vincent," Dan and I said in unison.

Vincent drove for a tow truck company that served our beat, so we saw him two or three times a week at accident scenes when he came to hook up smashed cars and sweep debris. Dan and had I commented for months about how weird looking he was and how strange he acted.

Vincent was tall, skinny, with rat-like brown hair, Coke-bottle glasses, and odd mannerisms usually exhibited by the creepy gardener in horror movies. While we had no evidence to implicate him in the murder, he simultaneously popped into our minds as a likely candidate.

Three days later, we got a call from the lead detective in the case. He said they had arrested Vincent on suspicion of murder. Although all the evidence they had uncovered in their investigation pointed at the weird man, he wasn't admitting anything. The detective said Vincent did acknowledge that he picked up the woman in his tow truck and drove her to South Stanton. Still, he couldn't remember anything after that.

The veteran detective didn't think he was faking his memory loss, so he would try something radical on the suspect—hypnosis.

He called us with news the following afternoon. Under hypnosis, Vincent admitted to killing the girl inside his tow truck. He told the hypnotist and the detectives that his sexual performance with the hooker wasn't his best, and she criticized him. Enraged, he grabbed her in a chokehold from behind, reached over her shoulder, and stabbed her chest with a screwdriver repeatedly.

Five times, the ME counted.

The hypnotist said the act of murder was so horrific to him that his conscious memory erased the incident at a point just moments before he had repeatedly stabbed her. Hypnosis brought that moment back.

The district attorney was victorious in court, and Vincent is now behind bars.

I wasn't involved in the homicide interview and the hypnosis phase, but I know Vincent's admission was a starting point for the detectives.

From thestudentlawyer.com, "The use of hypnosis in a criminal investigation."

"There is still debate amongst the scientific community as to whether hypnosis in itself actually exists. Nevertheless, and perhaps surprisingly, the police sometimes use hypnosis in the course of criminal investigations."

Confessing under hypnosis would likely have a defense attorney rubbing her palms together, anxious to cross-examine the detectives and the hypnotist. As of 2013, "there currently is no case law on the relevance of hypnosis evidence." From thestudentlawyer.com, "The use of hypnosis in criminal investigation."

But it can be used to garner information the police can use to assist in interviews and research.

This is similar to when the detectives told us they had narrowed the suspect to a tow truck driver or mechanic, and we simultaneously blurted, "Vincent." We said this, half in jest, based on how the man's appearance and mannerisms were like a movie actor's depiction of a creep. This wasn't enough for the detectives to arrest Vincent, but it gave them someone to look at, talk to, and so on. From that, the detectives would gather more tidbits and slowly—quickly in this instance—build their case. My partner and I never testified. There was no reason.

Hollywood lies about prostitution—there is nothing glamorous about it. That young, pretty girl working the corner for the first time won't look like that three months later. By then, she will have bruises, maybe a black eye, needle marks on her arms, and her personal hygiene will suffer.

Naïve girls and boys initially see prostitution as a way to make easy cash. I heard some variation of this many times from new hookers: "I do that stuff for my boyfriend, so I might as well do it for other dudes and make some easy money." They didn't know that drugs, assault, rapes, and violent pimps were also part of it. And murder too.

My partner and I did our best to protect them and, when they were accepting, help them get off the street.

We won some but lost more.

A WORD ON "ALMOST" MURDERS

I've been shot at a few times. Once is more than enough, especially when the incoming bullet buzzes by your ear like a really pissed-off bee.

Down by the river

There isn't anything like the sound of bullets ripping through tree limbs next to your head and smacking into tree trunks by your torso to make you run like an Olympic Games sprinter. I wasn't quite in my teens when one day a buddy and I were goofing around in a grove of trees next to the Columbia River that separates Oregon from Washington. It was a grey, misty day, and we were simply exploring, looking for treasures on the beach, and smoking cigarettes swiped from our parents, stuff we had done hundreds of times growing up by the river.

We hadn't seen anyone else on the beach, so when the first shot rang out from behind us, we were simultaneously startled and surprised. Falling pieces of leaves and bits of branches next to our heads underscored that the bullet was fired in our direction. Another gunshot and more falling debris launched us into an all-out run as multiple rounds buzzed by our young skulls. By the time we reached the road, our sniper had ceased.

We didn't tell our parents because they would have banned our treks to the river. Yeah, that was dumb.

At the police firing range

The second time a bullet missed me was when I was a range officer on the PD. Camp Withycombe, a few miles outside of Portland, let us use their firing ranges. One Friday night, after the shooters had all left, I told the other range officers to take off, and I would strip down the standing targets and tidy up.

The layout was somewhat typical for a firing range. There was a seven-foot dirt barrier on each side of the shooting area, a higher one behind the target silhouettes, and a small storage building on the other side of the left bank. An opening in the left bank near the front allowed passage to the building.

About 75 yards behind the range proper, a high cyclone fence separated the military facility from dozens and dozens of dilapidated mobile homes. Since the firing ranges were occupied every day of the week, day sleepers must have never slept. Perhaps it was one of those groggy and ticked off tenants who shot at me.

I had just picked up the last target and was about 10 feet from the passageway through the embankment when I heard a rifle shot and saw a chunk of earth rip free from the ground about four feet from me. Not wanting to know if he had another bullet, I charged into the passageway. Cellphones hadn't been invented yet, and there wasn't a landline in the storage building. So I tossed in the last silhouette, locked to the door, and darted from tree to tree to my car.

The shooter was never located.

Barricaded shooter

The third time, I was on the scene of a man barricaded in his apartment.

An officer had knocked on his door 30 minutes earlier regarding a noise complaint. A 60-year-old man jerked the door open and fired a round through the officer's hair. My partner and I were called to cover as well as a couple of other police units. We took position around the corner of the hall, about 30 feet from the door.

When negotiations failed, we decided to bring in the bomb robot to knock on the door and talk him out.

The robot was about four feet tall on wheels. It was equipped with a video camera, a speaker, and was controlled remotely. The plan was to send the robot up to the door, bump against it a few times (knock), and verbally order him out. The first couple of times failed to get a response. The third time, my partner and I duckwalked behind the robot, our guns drawn. It wasn't our wisest decision because the thing offered no more cover than would a skeleton.

We had learned that the shooter's name was Bob. As the robot rolled toward the door with us in its wake, the machine kept repeating, "Bob, come out. Bob, come out. Bob—"

Bob didn't come out, but he did fire through the wooden door. I don't remember how many rounds, but enough to shower us with metal shrapnel and a firestorm of sparks. Amazingly, we weren't hit with a bullet.

We sprinted down the hall and around the corner. Our very foolish attempt to get to the door could have been injurious or fatal. It was then and still is now one of those "What the hell were we thinking" moments.

Later that evening, our SWAT team crashed through Bob's outside window. When he tried to stab them with a butter knife, they disarmed him without injury.

The officer whose hair was parted never returned to work.

A plan disrupted

One day, a patrol car broadcasted a suspect car in a residential burglary near my location, a white over blue Ford with three occupants, one a female. Three minutes later, a Ford with the opposite color combination, blue over white, passed me going in the opposite direction with two occupants, both male. Reversed colors and missing a female, but my gut told me to check them out. Long story short, it was the right car, and there was a gun under the driver's seat. Nothing unusual about a secreted gun, but what I would learn later gave me pause.

To get a reduced sentence, the passenger testified against the driver. He told the district attorney, and later the jury, that as I approached the driver's side, the man behind the wheel whispered, "If the cop makes us [identifies them as the burglars], I'm putting a bullet in his head."

Happily, for my head, I got him out of the car before he had a chance to get the weapon.

In Saigon, Vietnam

American and Korean military vehicles got sniped from time to time when I was a military policeman in Saigon. The problem was that the insane traffic—motorbikes, military convoys, taxis, motorized pedicabs, and others—created a constant cacophony of ear-numbing sounds, making it impossible to hear a sniper's shot.

Today, I thank the poor marksmen who allowed me to return home from the war and each night from the police job in one piece. I'm sure there were other close calls I didn't know about. All officers have had them. Most cops accept the risk as part of their role as a sheepdog facing the wolves who want to do harm.

Does this make the sheepdog heroes or suckers? I've been called both, but I have never thought of the job either way. I chose it to be a protector and fight bullies in their every incarnation. What people called me was their opinion, which was none of my business. In other words, I never cared what they thought. I just did my best, and so did my fellow officers who had the same philosophy.

Here are three more almost murders.

CHAPTER 15

My Trainee

The bullet ripped through Dale's lower jaw, passed through his tongue, and lodged in a vertebra at the base of his neck. Four minutes later, his heart stopped.

Six minutes earlier, my trainee and I were searching for an armed man who had just robbed a liquor store and was last seen running toward a park. It was a scorching hot July 3rd in Portland, Oregon, so we knew picnickers were enjoying the rolling grounds and swimming pool.

Another officer came on the air and said he was at the park's parking lot entrance, and he had just spotted the suspect. Dale and I got there in less than a minute.

"He just went over that," the veteran officer said, pointing at a six-foot-high, 40-foot-long wooden fence around a residential home. "You guys take this location, and I'll go around the right end to block him from coming out that way."

Dale got out of the patrol car and moved quickly to the fence, and I ran toward its left end, where a broad, overgrown walnut tree with heavy branches drooped all the way to the ground. Just as I began to push through them, I heard a bang from the direction of our car.

Part of the fence must have fallen, I remember thinking. No, that was a gunshot. But it didn't sound like one, or did it? Maybe Dale shot the suspect. No, that wasn't a gun; it wasn't loud enough. Or was it?

In TV programs and movies, gunshots sound clearly like gunshots because the sound engineers make sure viewers enjoy the drama of a loud gunfight. Real-life shootings outside can be far more confusing.

This incident occurred before cell phones, and the PD wouldn't have individual portable radios for another year. Back then, officers were on their own until they could get to a landline, a car radio, or simply yell loud enough to get help.

I pushed deeper into the branches with one hand on the butt of my gun—and nearly bumped into a man who matched the suspect's description, moving through the branches toward me. His face was sweaty, and his eyes were shiny-crazed. In his hand, down along the side of his leg, he gripped a long-barrel revolver.

He raised it, seemingly slower than slow-motion, up, up, until I could see into the end of the black, yawning barrel. I saw his thumb sloooowly pulling back the hammer into the cocked position, the click louder than it should have been. I might have been confused about the bang I heard seconds earlier, but I knew what that click was.

Exceptional visual clarity for selected details, slow-motion time, and hearing distortions are typical in high-stress events. During this one, I experienced both diminished sound and intensified sound during the same situation. This is not uncommon. People can experience vivid perceptions of some details and miss others entirely.

I dove to the ground behind a Volkswagen Beetle and pointed my weapon up the side of the little car. After a moment of silence, I crawled along the car's length, then scooted up onto my knees next to the front fender. Hoping the suspect wasn't doing the same thing on the other side, I quick-peeked a couple of times over the sloped hood.

There he was, about 50 yards away in someone's backyard, standing next to a car with an open trunk lid.

He saw me, raised his gun, but I fired first.

The suspect spun in a half-circle and fell to the ground, landing on his belly. I heard shouting from the park, and out of the corner of my eye, I saw people running my way. I waved my hand in the universal gesture to get down and shouted, "Get down! Now!" For once, onlookers obeyed and dropped to the grass. I looked back toward my suspect.

He hadn't moved. I advanced toward him, my gun leading.

"Where are you hit?" I asked, jamming my gun barrel against his ear. The man's revolver lay in the grass a few feet away, its hammer still back.

"You missed me," the man groaned.

Later, I learned that my round had smacked into the upraised trunk lid next to his head. The sound of it hitting the metal fooled the suspect, at least for a second or two, into thinking he had been shot. When he realized the truth, it was too late to react because he saw me moving toward him. He wouldn't have gone far, anyway, because he had broken his ankle when he jumped over the fence.

As I was cuffing him, I heard a faint voice call "Loren" from across the yard. I looked about the yard, but I couldn't see him… There. Dale's head was just above the fence, his bloody hand holding his chin.

Absurdly, I thought he must have scraped his face trying to go over. I first refused to believe the bang I heard was a gunshot and then that the blood on Dale's face was from a bullet wound. Initial disbelief that something terrible has just happened is common.

Dale dropped out of sight.

A woman in a house across the street witnessed everything through her front window. She saw me run to the end of the fence, and Dale scoot over the top of it. She couldn't see the suspect who was crouched flush against the other side, pointing his gun upward, waiting. She probably heard the gunshot inside her home, but she wouldn't have known the bullet ripped through my trainee's chin. But she did see him fall off the fence into the tall grass, struggle to his feet, only to fall again. At this point, she saw blood pouring from his mouth and suspected what had happened.

She watched as he got up again, looked over the fence, waved (at me), and fell to the ground. Unable to get up, he crawled over to the police car and struggled across the passenger's seat to the mic.

Seeing an officer hurt, alone, and struggling to get help, the woman quickly called 911, told them what was going on and to send an ambulance.

The only thing other officers heard over the radio was Dale gurgling as blood pumped down his throat. Desperate, he managed to trip the siren before falling out of the car.

The officer covering the right side of the fence heard the shot and the siren and cautiously worked his way back through the trees to the scene. He shut off the siren, used the car radio to confirm that an ambulance was on the way, and comforted the recruit until the ambulance arrived.

As the EMTs worked on him, Dale's heart stopped for 45 seconds before their CPR efforts got it going again.

The woman's phone call saved the young officer's life.

The suspect, who smiled at me throughout the trial, was sentenced to a dozen years behind bars.

But he served only two and a half before being released.

My trainee had been on the job for only a few months; in fact, he had yet to go to the academy. I was his second coach. His first was a fine officer named Nick Meyers, whose story is told in Chapter 8, "Death of My Coach." Nick patrolled Northwest Portland and had been my coach when I took my four-month training tour at Central Precinct.

Dale was hospitalized for several days. He received hate mail while in the hospital, some letters hoping he was suffering, others wishing he had died, which he had for a few seconds. I was bitter about this, and I wondered if the job was worth it. That wasn't the first time I had had such thoughts; there would be many other times over the years that followed.

The doctors decided it was too dangerous to try to remove the bullet lodged against his upper vertebra. So it was left in place, which would cause him problems for years.

A few days later, I began hearing rumors that some officers said Dale shouldn't have gone over the fence since he couldn't see the other side. Hindsight is always 20/20, goes the old saying, meaning it's easy to know the right thing to do *after* something has happened. But cops went over fences all the time. If I had been on the passenger side, I would have gone over it since it was only 10 feet away. Dale simply scooted up and over, while I ran around it to hem the guy in.

But fate had a different plan.

Since I was his trainer, I called buddies at all the precincts and told them how the situation went down. One of them was Nick Meyers, Dale's last coach at Central Precinct and mine two years earlier. Nick was very happy to have gotten the straight scoop from me, especially since Dale and I were his graduates.

Nick would be murdered not long after.

Dale returned to work, but his neck bothered him, and his salivary glands were in bad shape. I protested when the leadership assigned him with me again. I had read enough about PTSD— and had some minor issues of my own from Vietnam—to know putting us together again wasn't a good idea. But the sergeants were grizzled old-school leaders. "Suck it up," they said, and that was that.

Dale's injuries forced him to take time off. He came back again but eventually retired due to his wounds.

A note to gun enthusiasts. Before this shooting, I had a problem at the firing range pulling my shots to the left. So I spent extra time shooting to correct the problem. Finally, after a few weeks, I was shooting straight.

Or so I thought. As the saying goes, "Everyone has a plan until they get punched in the face."

The stress of shooting at a live target negated my recent fix, and I once again pulled my shot.

The solution? Practice more until the problem goes away, even under stress-shooting exercises.

CHAPTER 16

The Warning

Police officers and just about anyone with experience in the realm of violence understand the concept of "I had a gut feeling." I had my share of them in the Vietnam War and on the city streets as a cop.

But on one occasion—a pleasant afternoon in August—the feeling was different because it came at me out of the blue when I was engaged in a no-big-deal traffic stop.

Let me illustrate the difference between what is considered a typical gut feeling in police work and what I experienced on that summer day. The previous winter, other officers and I responded to an armed robbery of a veterinarian hospital where staff and customers, including an off-duty cop, were forced into a large dog cage. The cop was carrying his weapon, but he was quickly overpowered and disarmed.

As we arrived at the hospital, dispatch told us that the armed holdup men had fled out the back door. One officer went into the animal hospital to gather information; the rest of us began a coordinated search of the back lot and the connecting backyards to private residences.

There were several stacked kennels in the lot, waist-high weeds, two sheds, and an old garage. This occurred before cops called SWAT for every little thing, so the three of us searched the kennels, the small buildings, and behind a six-foot-high wooden fence surrounding the lot.

As we searched, I had an intense sensation that someone was watching us. This wasn't an unusual feeling because it fell within the parameters of the situation.

Our search ended when police units checking side streets around the hospital informed dispatch that they had caught the suspects. The holdup men subsequently admitted to hiding in a garage loft in the next yard over, a place from which they could see our movements as we searched.

Again, there was nothing supernatural about feeling watched because we were at the scene of a crime just moments after the suspects had fled.

But it was a different situation on that August afternoon in a tree-lined residential area. The day was beginning to heat up, and the neighborhood streets were quiet, probably because anyone not at work was staying inside out of the sun. There was no other traffic, no barking dogs, not even a chirping bird. Just quiet.

When a motorist blew through a stop sign as if it were a green light, I pulled him over in front of a two-story white house. I never liked writing citations, figuring a simple stop and a warning was good enough to get most drivers' heads out of wherever they had been and back on the task of paying attention to the road. The driver was pleasant, apologetic, and he even thanked me.

That's when I felt it.

My heart rate suddenly accelerated, and a tingling sensation danced up my spine to bristle the fine hairs at the base of my neck. I'd felt this often in Vietnam, and at least once a week on high-risk situations on the police job, like kicking in a door on a dangerous warrant service or approaching a man with a gun. But on a pleasant summer day on a sleepy street? I bid the driver a good day and watched him pull away from the curb.

The feeling remained. If it hadn't been the traffic stop giving me the heebie-jeebies, then what…?

I made a 360-degree turn, scanning the sidewalks in all directions. I noted the streets as far as I could see north, south, west, and east, and I looked at the big house I was parked in front of and at the ones on each side of it. Nothing, and I didn't see anything suspicious with those on the other side of the street. So why was my adrenalin accelerating?

With the fight/flight juices percolating in my veins and with no one with whom to battle and no threat to back away from, I headed back to my car. But before I could get there, the feeling worsened. My heart was thumping now, my eyes watering, and goosebumps were popping out on my arms.

I had to get in the car and do so quickly.

A lot of officers refer to their police units as their "office." Some think of their car as a protective shield against threats and dangers from forces outside of it. This is an illusion because the car doesn't protect against much of anything other than the weather. In fact, it makes for a larger target. Officers know this, but they still take some comfort once they slip inside and shut the door.

But getting into my car didn't alleviate any of the feelings. I again scanned all four sides. Nothing. Not until I accelerated away from the curb did the sensation begin to lessen. Two blocks away, I pulled under the shade of a big tree and sat to let my heart rate return to normal, my anxiety decrease, and my adrenaline cool.

Eventually, I returned to patrol, and my shift ended three hours later without incident. The next day my sergeant asked me to see him after roll call.

"You stop a car on Sixty-Third at Fleet yesterday?" he asked.

"I know nothing, and I wasn't even there," I said with a smirk. When the sergeant didn't smile at the old police alibi, I told the sergeant I had. "Guy blew a stop sign, and I gave him a verbal. He complaining?" I didn't understand why he would file a complaint. I was pleasant to him and—

"You stop him in front of a white house, a big one, two stories?"

"I didn't block their driveway. Did the owner..." Then I remembered the terrible case of the creeps I'd had on the traffic stop. More accurately, the rush of dread I'd had after it.

"Better sit down," the sergeant said. "A young woman came into the precinct last night. Said a uniform officer was in front of her house yesterday afternoon talking to a driver. Said her fiancé has a real hate-on for the cops; he's an ex-con."

"Okay," I said, wondering where this was going.

"He saw you through the window, and apparently, he flipped out. Told his girlfriend he was going to shoot you. He retrieved a rifle, loaded it, and propped the barrel on a windowsill. He lined you up in his sights and was about to fire when the woman leaped at him and tried to get the rifle away. You drove off while they were rolling around fighting on the floor. The ex-con got the weapon back, but he was majorly upset that you had left. So he beat his girlfriend pretty badly. She got away, and that's when she came here to the precinct."

I slumped deep into the chair, struggling for air.

"Close one," the sergeant said with a shake of his head. "Be careful out there. You just used up your good karma."

Surviving the cop-hating ex-con was a combination of interference from the soon-to-be ex-girlfriend and a gift from the paranormal. Some argue that there is no such thing as a sixth sense; there is only a heightening of the five. But in this case, there were no indicators for my other senses to alert on. I didn't *hear* a bullet chambered. I didn't *see* the couple fighting. And I didn't *smell, feel,* or *taste* anything tangible.

One time, I got assigned to work with a trainee who had trouble adapting to the mean streets. She was a recent graduate from a very liberal college with a master's degree in biology. There had been an incident with her last coach where a man threatened them with a whirring chainsaw. As the coach stood behind a car fender with his gun pointing at the threat, he looked back to check on his trainee. Imagine his surprise to see her leaning against the side of the police car, filing her nails. Yes, you read that right.

At one point during our time together, she said, "I just can't wrap my mind around the fact that people I don't even know want to hurt me because I'm a police officer."

I never had that confusion. I came home from a war with a complete understanding that people, most of a country, to name a few, wanted to hurt me. And by the time the cop-hating ex-con tried to snipe me out of a window, I had about eight years on the job and knew very well that lots and lots of people wanted a piece of me.

So I was always alert and aware.

But this situation was different. What I felt that day was a warning from... I don't know.

CHAPTER 17

Almost An Officer-Involved Shooting

Dispatch said a man was running through the halls of a hotel screaming and waving a gun around.

We met the front desk clerk, who said he hadn't seen the guy for the last few minutes and thought he might have gone back to his third-floor room. He gave us the key. We took the stairs in the event the man might be hiding in the stairwell. He wasn't.

There wasn't an answer when we knocked on the door to his room. We used the key and executed a tactical entry. Empty. We found a .38 cal. gun and a box of ammunition under the mattress. But the timeline of events, according to the witness, indicated the man had a second pistol.

The counterman appeared at the door. "He's out in the parking lot," he said, his voice quivering. "Just outside the glass doors to the back lot." He didn't know if the man was still armed.

My partner and I took the elevator down to the lobby. A small crowd had gathered at the glass doors looking out into the parking lot. "The guy is loony," a maid said. "He scared me when he ran up and down the halls waving a pistol."

We got everyone to back away from the glass doors, then quick-peeked outside.

The rain was pounding down as if the parking lot were under a great waterfall. The allegedly armed man in question was standing in the open about 50 feet from the doors, bare-chested, his bare feet together, his arms extended out from his sides in a crucifix pose. Rain streamed through his long hanging hair and cascaded down his body.

My partner and I slipped out the doors and took cover behind a sedan parked a few feet away from the doors. We draped our arms across the hood and trunk and centered our gunsights on him.

So hard was the rain beating down, it was difficult to see him clearly, and I had to shout twice for him to hear me identify ourselves. I gave him the usual commands to put his hands behind his head and turn around, but he refused, smiling as if happy we were there. His hands were empty, but the rain prevented us from seeing if there was a bulge in his pockets. Nor could we see the small of his back.

Another officer took up position behind a parking structure post off to the man's right. He radioed that he couldn't see if there was a weapon in his pockets, but his rear waistband appeared not to hold a gun.

The man maintained the crucifix pose as he slowly tilted his head back, letting the rain pound his face. He screamed unintelligibly at the heavens, then lowered his head, looked at us, and slowly began to drop his arms. "Keep your hands up!" my partner shouted, but the man ignored the command. He grinned at us, and his shoulders shook as if he was chuckling. His descending left arm stopped at a 45-degree downward angle, but his right hand continued to drop toward his pocket.

That's when I knew: *I'm going to have to shoot him.*

I looked behind us and saw that people had gathered inside behind the glass doors again. If the man shot at us and missed, he would likely hit them; I gestured for the people to get away from the doors. They didn't. "We have to move away from here," I told my partner, though there was no other cover available.

The man kept moving his right hand toward his pocket.

Officers are trained to aim at a threat's mass because there is less chance of a miss than shooting at an arm or leg. A missed shot means the bullet continues to travel until something or someone stops it. We could see people in the parking structure behind him walking about.

I'm going to have to send a bullet into his heart, I thought. *There is no way out of this.* My adrenaline was pumping, and my heart rate was in the red zone. *I don't want to shoot him. I don't want that in my head for the rest of my life. Don't make me shoot you—*

He moved his right hand closer toward his pocket. "Keep your hand away from your pocket!" my partner shouted. I looked behind us; the people had moved away from the doors.

The downpour increased, as powerful as the monsoons in Asia. Defying my partner, the man moved his hand even closer to his pocket, then away from it a couple of inches. He shouted something, then chuckled, his shoulders bumping up and down.

He plunged his hand into his pocket. "I'm shooting him," my partner said. I was already squeezing the trigger on my revolver.

The man yanked his hand out, tilted his head back, and snapped both arms out to his sides, again in the crucifixion pose. "Matches," a voice on the radio said. It was the officer behind the pillar. "He pulled out books of matches."

I eased off the trigger, my hand trembling.

The third officer streaked out from behind his cover and whipped his baton across the man's knees, sending him splattering down onto the flooded pavement. He fought a little, but we quickly got him into handcuffs.

I felt … I didn't know what I was feeling. In the beginning, I was hoping I wouldn't have to shoot the man. I didn't want to take a mentally ill person's life, nor did I want his death in my psyche for the rest of my life. Then my thinking shifted to accepting that I would have to.

Given the totality of the situation—the man's bizarre behavior before and after we arrived, multiple witnesses seeing a gun, finding a gun and ammo in his room, movements typical of someone reaching for a weapon—I knew I was only seconds away from killing him.

I was justified because the situation was such that my action—a simple squeeze of the trigger—was necessary. If I had shot, would I be exonerated? I would undoubtedly be made a monster by the media and cop critics. But a wise grand jury would see my actions as reasonable.

Officers often don't have time for reflection when presented with a deadly threat. The moment explodes, and shots ring out. But in this situation, we were being toyed with minute after minute. My emotions were on a wild roller coaster ride: not wanting to hurt the man, concern for bystanders, acceptance of the threat, then permitting myself to do what needed to be done. My adrenaline was pumping, my mind was focused, and I was ready to go.

Then, abruptly, it didn't happen.

Suddenly, a new roller coaster ride: I felt intensely keyed up, a sense of something left undone, but a huge relief, and happy I didn't have to shoot him. It's an understatement to say that it was a confusing and uncomfortable set of emotions that lasted for several days. I had many other situations like this, including one in which a man shot at me. The feelings were similar but not as intense as this event.

What surprised me was how the situation left me feeling. I didn't have to shoot the guy, but I couldn't shake the feeling of a chair being yanked away as I was about to sit. If you've had someone do that to you with a chair, you know it's a shock both physically and mentally.

With the man in the rain, the abruptness of the moment's cessation was jarring and hard on my mind and body.

I've shot at people, but this experience in the rain and a few other similar ones impacted me harder than those times I completed the trigger pull.

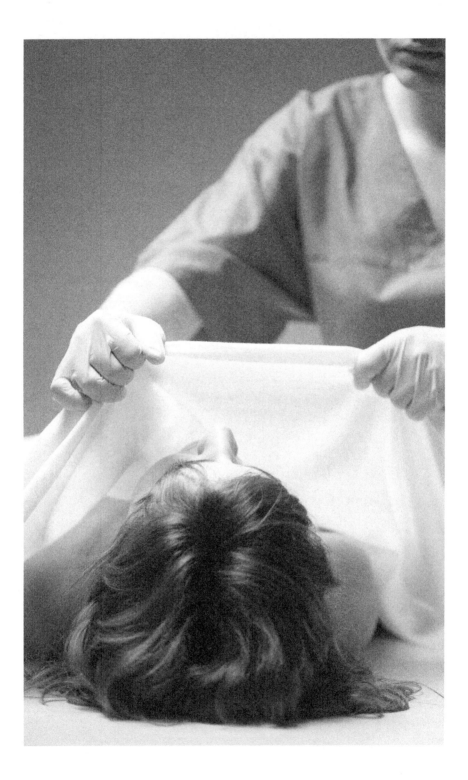

SECTION TWO

SUICIDES

So often in police work, officers arrive at a scene like moviegoers walking into a theater halfway through the film. What's going on? Who are the players here? Why are these two people so upset? And whose blood is that on the floor?

With a suicide call, it's as if the officer walked into the movie when "The End" appears on the screen, pun not intended. It's clear to the officers what happened. Still, there might not be direct evidence as to why the deceased decided to end it all. Did he have health issues? A broken heart? Lose his job? Did he exhaust all possibilities before implementing the final solution? Did he factor in how his death would affect people who cared about him?

I can't recall any suicide I covered that occurred amid a crowd or even around three or four people. All took place when the victim was alone. The decision was perhaps contemplated for weeks, months, even years, or possibly it was a snap one. I had no idea because all I had was the dead victim and one or two people who discovered the deceased. Sometimes the discoverers knew the person, friend, fellow employee, or relative. Other times, the victims were found by an apartment manager or a stranger.

My job was to examine the body and the scene for evidence of a crime, gather statements and IDs from those at the scene, call for a detective if the death looked suspicious, ask dispatch to send my supervisor, and finally call the morgue to collect the body. If the body had been found by relatives, I treated them with sensitivity and compassion, while at the same time getting information for my report and keeping a suspicious eye out for anything that didn't look right. That was often a challenge.

There wasn't time to feel any kind of emotion for those who had just made the most significant and most final decision of their lives. A cop can't do their job if they are overcome emotionally at any type of call.

Later, when I was back in the car or having a coffee, I'd reflect on the incident. Sometimes, the method of death was so gory, I'd only think of that and wonder how long the image would remain in my mind. Other times, I'd wonder what led up to the person's decision.

Such pondering was usually short-lived as dispatch always had another call to send me to. At times, not having a moment to collect myself was difficult. If my next call was a minor theft or maybe a loud music complaint, it could be a challenge to focus on the new problem when the suicide victim's dead face was still in the forefront of my mind.

I often thought about the traumatized loved ones who sometimes would never find out what was troubling the victims.

While I never investigated a suicide that occurred around others, I knew of one where a man killed his wife and himself in the presence of their two young children. His father wanted him to have a military funeral, but everyone balked. He might have been depressed and had other mental issues, but he was also a murderer. He killed his wife.

My dad had a life-long friend named Terry. They went through the depression together, shelling walnuts to make a living during those difficult times. As their lives improved with marriage, kids, and full-time jobs, they remained close, and I can remember us doing things together as families.

The day before I left home to fly to Vietnam, Terry stuck a .30-06 hunting rifle in his mouth and blew his brains all over his little camper.

My dad told his wife that he would come over and clean up the mess, but first, he had to take me to the airport so I could go to war.

As it's often said, "Suicide doesn't take away the pain; it gives it to someone else."

CHAPTER 18

Saigon, Vietnam
A Hanging

I got assigned a new partner, bookish and fleshy from New York City, where he had been a chemist. Uncle Sam drafted Elmer right after he had made some new discovery. He sarcastically said that the Army apparently figured his years working with test tubes made him a perfect fit for the military police. We liked each other right off, and we worked together a few times. Still, I was never comfortable with his ability in bar brawls and foot chases since he hadn't even been in a schoolyard scuffle.

Our first radio call was a suicide, an American civilian man found in a shed behind a bar.

A crowd had gathered outside the dilapidated building, some of them pointing at the door, repeatedly saying, *"Chet chet chet,"* meaning "dead dead dead." There were no lights inside the structure, which was about the size of a one-car garage, but enough leaked in through the open door and a small, grimy window to see the man hanging from a rafter. His face was purplish, his tongue hung out, and, judging by his stretched neck, he had been hanging there for a while. He wore dark clothing, and he had voided himself all over the kicked-over chair.

Shakespeare said, "Many a good hanging prevents a bad marriage." My guess, based on other incidents I had handled with American civilians, was he had been fired from his job and had insufficient money to fly home. His misery ultimately affected his rational thinking, and he determined that killing himself was his best option.

I turned to say something to Elmer, but he wasn't there. A kid standing in the doorway pointed outside and said, *"di-di,"* Vietnamese slang for "go quick." I worked my way through the laughing crowd to find Elmer leaning on the Jeep fender, retching his morning chow into the dirt road.

"You, okay?" I asked, just to be funny.

"That man… awful," he managed, wiping the back of his hand across his mouth.

Yes, it was awful. Seeing a man's neck turn into one that looked like a giraffe's was hard to take. This was my first hanging, too, but I recognized that it was essential to continue to do our job, no matter how unpleasant the visual. The hanging was a low-keyed death, and we had the luxury of stepping outside for a deep inhalation of relatively fresh air. Other situations wouldn't allow that option.

My psychology 101 was that Elmer needed to have his face shoved in it, figuratively speaking. So, I grabbed his arm and led him back into the shed.

He didn't like me forcing him, but he stayed inside and did his job. He was an okay MP during our times working together.

About a week before I went into the Army, I was walking with a buddy when we came upon a terrible car accident—people down, blood all about, smoking twisted metal. My friend stopped 50 feet back and wanted to take another route, but I went forward to force myself to see the carnage. I thought it valuable to toughen up to the visual. I did the same thing during my first two years in the Army stateside. While others looked away from pain and suffering, I got up close to it.

While this might sound sick, I was practicing a form of mental imagery, also called mental rehearsal. I've studied a lot on the subject over the years since, and I've written about it in magazine pieces and two books. It's a powerful tool in which a person repeatedly images in detail the sight, sound, smell, taste, and feel of an event or activity. Countless studies show that mental imagery is so powerful that people can use it to practice sports, public speaking, police and military tactics, and many other activities to maintain their skill level and progress.

In my case, I would deliberately expose myself to unpleasant imagery and see myself functioning in it. While my experiences in Vietnam were different from what I had imaged up until then, there were enough similarities that my mental toughening helped me not freeze when exposed to visual horrors and proceed to do my job.

Note: The term "visualization" refers to *seeing* an action in your mind's eye. "Mental imagery" involves experiencing an action with all the senses, *seeing, feeling, hearing, touching, and smelling.* Mental imagery is a more powerful technique that gets superior results.

CHAPTER 19

Death By Autoerotic Asphyxiation Hanging

My training coach and I got a call on a suicide in a low-rent apartment building. We met the complainant, the manager, and followed him to the grungy fourth-floor room. The victim was hanging from an exterior pipe that ran across the ceiling in the one-room apartment. A chair lay on its side under his dangling feet.

The man, early 20s, was wearing a woman's bra and pantyhose. We determined that after he laid out a dozen or so pornographic pictures on the floor, he stood on the chair to tie one end of a set of stockings over the 8-inch in diameter pipe and the other around his neck.

This happened early in my police career when I hadn't heard of autoerotic asphyxiation: an accidental death that occurs during sexual self-stimulation. Between 70 to 80 percent of the deaths are caused by hanging. Ten to 30 percent are attributed to plastic bags slipped over the head and tightly secured at the neck. People who practice autoerotic asphyxiation derive a sense of sexual arousal from a lack of oxygen to the brain. Death by asphyxia occurs by accident.

The man in the apartment had likely kicked over his chair while in the throes of sexual pleasure.

Apparently, my training coach hadn't heard of the practice either, as he didn't utter a word about it. So I wrote up the incident as a suicide, leaving out what the man was wearing and the porno pics. I did this in case his family obtained a copy of the report.

About three weeks later, one of the sergeants found me in the locker room and said a man, woman, and teenage girl were in the lobby wanting to talk to me. He said, "It's about the boy who hung himself." I asked if my coach could do it, and he said I wrote the report, so it was my responsibility.

The family was distraught and wanted answers. They were from the mid-west and said their son was hiking around the country to have an adventure. He seemed perfectly fine when they last talked with him during his regular call-in. He wasn't despondent, depressed, or exhibiting any of the other elements of a potential suicide.

I decided not to tell them the kinky stuff. I said that their son had hung himself from a pipe in the apartment. There were no signs of drug usage or foul play. They asked if he left a note, and I said he hadn't.

The information seemed to make them more distressed than before. The family didn't understand why or how he could kill himself since there hadn't been a single indicator of a problem. They thanked me and headed back to home.

It wouldn't be until later after I learned about autoerotic asphyxiation that I regretted not telling the family the complete story. Because of my embarrassment and my not wanting them to feel the same, I misled them. No doubt, I left them thinking they had somehow not picked up on their son's psychological problems and thus missed an opportunity to help him.

My excuse is that I was young, new, and ignorant. But it still bothers me today that I hurt the family even more than they already were.

CHAPTER 20

A Bathtub Autoerotic Asphyxiation Hanging

This one came a few years after the autoerotic asphyxia in which the young man hung himself from a pipe in his apartment. I knew a little more about the phenomenon this time, though it was only my second case.

This one involved a 30-year-old man hanging himself from his bathtub faucet while lying in a tub of water. He was naked, lying on his back, the water nearly to the top, with a makeshift noose around his neck. The usual signs of strangulation were present: crimson face and a protruding tongue.

Unlike the rope the man in Vietnam used and the pantyhose the victim employed around the ceiling pipe, the noose used in the tub was short since the faucet was attached to the tub's rim. The victim's head was above the water when found by the family and when I arrived on the scene. So he didn't drown.

The family was distraught and confused. "Why would he take his life?" they kept asking. "He was so young, he had a job, and he had a girlfriend." Not one of them considered that his death was an accident, the result of autoerotic asphyxia taken too far.

The medical examiner was on the way, so I decided to let him give them the news if that was indeed the cause of death.

According to an article "Autoerotic Asphyxiation Paraphilia: When Self-Pleasuring Becomes Self-Destruction: Autoerotic Asphyxiation Paraphilia," by Andrew P. Jenkins, Ph.D., CHES,

EMT Central Washington University, "Autoerotic asphyxia (AEA), the practice of using strangulation to enhance the pleasure of masturbating, annually claims the lives of between 250 and 1,000 young American men."

Females dying from autoerotic asphyxiation are rare, but it does happen. The youngest to die was age 9, the oldest 89. The average age is 33. Source: Coronertalk.com

CHAPTER 21

Almost A Tree Hanging

One summer evening, I was patrolling in a Southeast Portland neighborhood when a woman ran out from between two houses, waving frantically at me. "There's a guy with a noose around his neck hanging from a tree branch behind this white house." I told dispatch and let the woman lead the way.

Sure enough, a man was dangling as the end of a rope, his feet about six feet above the ground. One of his legs twitched.

"He's still alive," I said, encircling my arms around his thighs and lifting to remove the weight from his neck. He was big and heavy, so I called a couple of onlookers to quickly climb the tree and untie the rope. They did, and we were able to lower the man to the grass.

By now, he had regained consciousness enough to realize his suicide attempt had been interrupted. This ticked him off, which he demonstrated by kicking at me. We grappled for a bit until I managed to get him into handcuffs. My backup helped me wrestle him to my car and into my backseat.

I drove him to one of the hospitals we used for people mentally ill enough to harm themselves or others.

I never heard anything more about him. I hope he was able to get his life in order.

Police detectives and other investigators sometimes spent weeks, months, and even years with people involved with a case. As a result, the investigator developed a relationship with the participants. This could be a good or bad thing, depending on the situation.

Uniformed officers were usually in the participant's lives for just a few minutes, though on rare occasions longer. When it came to a dead body call, officers talked to people, consoled them, arranged for a medical examiner to pick up the body, or ordered an ambulance when the suicide failed. Then the officers were off to the next call.

Sometimes, it felt strange to me to be present at the end of a person's life, perform my required duties at the scene, then leave. Sometimes this would take only 30 minutes, sometimes longer, on rare occasions, less. In short, someone's life ended, I showed up for a few, then left.

It always seemed like my time on the scene should have been longer, that I should have done something else to underscore the significance of the end of a life.

On the flip side, there were times when I showed up at a natural death when family and friends were confused and even angry about why I was called there. Even after I explained that we had to come on all unwitnessed deaths, they were still upset.

CHAPTER 22

Motorcycle Chase

I was nearing the end of my 18-month rookie probation and working downtown with a coach. We were more partners than trainee-coach, but skid row was such a different world than other parts of the city, I didn't mind the guidance from a veteran. It was about 10 o'clock at night when dispatch announced to all the downtown cars that they had received several calls about a motorcyclist traveling at a high rate of speed heading toward the city.

"I was about to tell y'all I was behind him," came Cody's drawl over the radio. He was a good ol' boy with college degrees.

"He's nearin' a hundred miles per hour and looks like he's drinkin' from a bottle of liquor."

"Is he coming into the city?" an officer asked over the radio.

"I'm guessin' that's the case. He's got a choice to make in a second, City Center or the bridge to the east side... Okay, he took the City Center exit and took another swig from his bottle. He sure can handle his motorcycle. He's down to ninety now."

My coach was driving. "He's going to come out by PSU," he said, goosing us up Broadway toward the freeway exits that dump traffic into the city. "We'll block Fourth Avenue."

Cory's voice had gone up a couple of octaves. "He's goin' down Second, hittin' sixty-five and chuggin' from his bottle and blowin' through every intersection."

"How did he get there so quickly?" my coach shouted over our siren, sliding us around the next intersection then accelerating toward Second.

"He turned west on Yamhill," Cory blared, "damn near laid it down—and now he took a hard left on Third and headin' south. He's doing fifty or so."

Other police units came on the air giving their location.

Cody's voice was screeching like a bad violin now. "He's goin' down Fourth now— He just clipped a couple of parked cars, but he didn't lose it. Diiii-am!"

One of our criminalists, driving a large white van, had just finished fingerprinting a crime scene. He decided to park at Third Avenue, two blocks from Portland State University, and be ready to use the van to block the intersection.

My coach was flooring us south on Fourth.

"Okay," Cody shouted, "He just cornered onto Fifth Avenue. Nearly lost it. He's acceleratin' hard…. Fifty…sixty…"

The criminalistics investigator heard Cody's broadcast and dropped his shift into Drive.

"I think I saw the motorcycle ahead of us," my coach shouted over the siren. We were still on Fourth Avenue. "Look four intersections up. There! Did you see him rip through it?"

I did. But the chase car said he was on Fifth Avenue heading toward PSU. The chase was so fast that by the time someone announced the motorcycle's location, it was changing to a new one.

Two blocks up, the Criminalistics van was just starting to enter the Fourth Avenue intersection. He was looking ahead at the Fifth Avenue crossing, hoping to get there in time to block the street. He was halfway across when the speeding motorcycle T-boned him.

We were two blocks away with our siren blaring so we couldn't hear the explosion, but we saw the brilliant flash followed by a mini mushroom cloud rising high above the street. My coach spewed a string of expletives and slowed us as we neared the intersection.

I took in the awful sight in a series of quick visual snapshots.

◇ The motorcycle, about 15 feet away from a white van's caved-in side door, lay collapsed like the bellows of an accordion.

◇ Large flames engulfed the motorcycle and the pavement around it.

- ✧ The driver lay sprawled a few feet away, also consumed by fire.

- ✧ A man, it took me a moment to recognize him as one of our criminalists, was pulling the motorcyclist by his boot away from flames.

- ✧ The man's burning head appeared to be nearly twice the size of what was normal.

- ✧ His helmet popped off his head.

- ✧ A bottle of liquor lay a few away, unbroken. Cherry vodka.

My coach spoke softly. "It looks like the front wheel of his motorcycle hit the van first, which catapulted the driver. See the small dent above the big one? That's from his head."

I couldn't get over how quickly his head had swelled. That and the two fires—the motorcycle and the man—was a bit much to absorb.

The Criminalist was clearly shaken. "I heard he was on Fifth Avenue. So I was heading over to the intersection to try to block him or slow him down. He..." He shook his head, lost for words.

"He was on Fifth," my coach said, patting his back. "But he cut over to Fourth. The guy wanted to die. If it had been a weekday instead of a Sunday, he would have hurt or killed a lot of people."

The driver was a teenager, though no one could see that during the chase or when he lay burning. It wouldn't have made a difference anyway because he needed to be stopped before he hurt someone or himself. The boy's father came to the police station and explained that his son had been drinking cherry vodka from the bottle all evening and said he wanted to kill himself. The father assured us he didn't hold a grudge against the police. "You did what you had to do to protect innocent people," he said.

Suicide by cop is quite common. Fortunately, no officers or citizens were hurt in this incident, though the crash was a block short of a busy university. However, a criminalist was traumatized, and chase officers were left with a permanent mental image.

CHAPTER 23

Suicide By Rifle

I got a death by suicide call. A firearm, she added. I was working alone, and it was nearing midnight. The two-story house was in a quiet residential area, lit by flashing lights from an ambulance and a neighboring beat car that responded to cover me if the gun became an issue.

As I stepped through the front door, the victim was slumped into an easy chair against the left living room wall. His head was back against the chair, his face angled upward as if looking at the ceiling, his brains making a large splatter pattern on the wall behind him. The backup officer stood next to the rifle on the floor below the victim's hanging arm.

The man's girlfriend was hysterical. We would learn that she had recently ended their relationship, which he took hard, real hard. She came to his house after he called her, threatening to take his life. When he didn't answer the door, she used her key to enter and found him as I did a few minutes later.

Dispatch told me the medical examiners were having a busy night, so they couldn't pick up the deceased for a while. How long, they couldn't estimate. Though this wasn't unusual, it was never good news.

My backup volunteered to take the weapon to the property room for me. The girlfriend left with her sister, and the ambulance crew left too.

For an hour and a half, I sat with the dead man. He was sprawled awkwardly in the plush chair, and I was on a sofa perpendicular to him. There was a large picture window that provided a view of my police car and street. Few vehicles passed so late.

It was past the end of my shift now. It had been a busy night, and though I brought a sandwich and a container of yogurt from home, I only managed to stuff down the sandwich as I was rushing to a call. I wanted the yogurt, but it was in a bag on my front seat.

I couldn't remember if bureau policy prohibited my leaving the scene, even briefly. But I was starving, and the people who wrote the rule book weren't around.

I retrieved the yogurt and a plastic spoon, then hurried up the steps and back into the house. I looked over at the victim, his mouth blasted open, the still-dripping mess on the wall behind him, then back down at my yogurt container. Strawberry.

I hadn't thought this through. Was I going to sit on the sofa 10 feet away from and spoon strawberry yogurt into my mouth? Had I gotten so callous in only four years on the bureau and a year in Vietnam?

I went back out on the porch and stood in front of the plate-glass window. That way, I could have a snack and keep an eye on the victim.

*

Cops, funeral directors, firefighters, and hospital staff must approach the sight of death in their own way. What works for one person might not work for another. My way was to make myself look at the deceased and observe every nuance. My motivation was to toughen myself up so I could function. Did it work? I think so, with one exception. I could never bring myself to touch a dead body. It was my quirk, and fortunately, I never had to. Well, there was once. The deceased man's leg was extended into a pathway where cops, firemen, and EMTs were rushing by. So that no one tripped over him, I used my foot to nudge his leg out of the way. That was quite an accomplishment for me.

I read about a man who wanted to be a career EMT. He felt that he should do something to prepare himself, so he took a job in a funeral home. He didn't have the credentials to work on bodies, but he could pick up the deceased at a scene or hospital. He also volunteered to help with preparing bodies for funerals and with embalming. Because his experiences toughened him to the sights and smell of the deceased, he now advises other people who want a career in the field to first work in the funeral business.

The more gruesome cases, I found, often had an unreality about them. They didn't compute in my head as true but instead created by Hollywood for a slasher movie. That impression was always brief as the hubbub—sirens, EMTs, firetrucks, screaming friends and relatives—quickly brought me back to the harsh reality.

CHAPTER 24

Another Suicide By Rifle

The Wayne family was well-known to the Portland Police. Mom and dad had raised a bevy of burglars, dopers, armed robbers, and assaulters. And we could count on them fighting us no matter how minor the contact.

My partner and I were working the night shift in Northeast Portland when dispatch called our number. *"Suicide by firearm. Be advised, it's the Wayne family home. The vic is Stanley."*

Dispatch knew him, and we did too.

There were a lot of cars parked out front. Did they come after the suicide, or were they already present when it happened? The front door was closed, but we could hear lots of yelling before getting out of the car. When someone opened the door and came out, we quickly slipped in without asking. Given it was the Wayne's, there was a good possibility it could be a homicide.

The living room was gloomy, with only one corner lamp struggling against total darkness. The yelling had stopped, leaving only the sound of wailing from a heavy-set woman on the couch. About a dozen people glared at us without uttering a word. Someone bent down and said something to the howling woman. We learned later she was the victim's mother.

She might have been large enough to fill half the sofa, but she sprang up faster than anyone her age and size should have been capable of, pushed a woman out of her way, and grabbed the butt of my partner's gun. He didn't see her because he was sidestepping a shoulder ram from an angry man to his right.

This was before we got specialized safety holsters that require a subtle move by the officer to extract the weapon.

Mrs. Wayne had pulled my partner's gun halfway out of the holster when I slammed my palm into her chest, sending her reeling backward and down onto the sofa.

That got everyone's attention.

"Where is Stanley?" my partner asked.

Fingers pointed toward a dark hall. "Last door on the right," someone said.

We flipped on the hall light and moved stealthily down the hall. We kept glancing behind us should there be more threats from the living room while at the same time watching the multiple closed doors in the event someone sprang out. We reached the last door without incident and pushed it open.

Stanley lay crumpled on the floor at the foot of his bed, the side of his mouth blown apart, a rifle lying next to his open hand. We checked around the room for drugs, legal and illegal, and a suicide note. Nothing. Two detectives came in the room, nodded at us, and surveyed the scene. "Anything look off to you guys?" one of them asked us.

We told them we had just arrived and explained that things were tense in the living room. But at first blush, it looked like Stanley was sitting at the end of his bed, put the butt of the rifle on the floor, probably between his legs, his mouth over the barrel, and pulled the trigger. The detectives nodded and went out into the living room to talk to people.

The medical examiners came in. No matter how often I saw it done, I never got used to seeing one of them shove a latex-covered finger into a bullet hole and move it around like a swizzle stick in a cocktail. Sometimes they found the bullet; other times, they didn't.

After a few minutes of poking, prodding, and turning the body this way and that, one of them declared that it was a suicide.

My partner and I acted as security as they carried the stretcher with Stanly Wayne zipped up in a body bag through the house filled with cranky people and out the front door. We took possession of the rifle to place in our property room. Once the MEs had loaded him into their van, they chatted with us for a few minutes out in the street.

One of them had a walrus-sized mustache that nearly covered his mouth. He was laughing about something my partner said when I noticed he was still wearing the latex gloves. The right one, his finger probe hand, was still bloody with small chunks on the end of his finger. He was in the middle of telling a story when he reached up with his right hand and scratched his big mustache— leaving a pink piece of what had to be brain matter in the hairs.

I looked at my partner, and he looked at me, our subtle expressions asking the same thing: Should we tell him?

We made a subtle shake of our heads, then continued listening to the man's story, though distracted by that bobbing chunk of whatever.

Later in the car, I asked, "You think we should have told him?"

"No," he said, "but if it's still there on our next dead body, we should probably let him know."

It's not surprising that the emotions of friends and family at the scene of death are often through the roof. Sometimes traumatized and angry friends and family members followed the medical examiners' van carrying the deceased to their office. When things got tense or physically combative at the morgue, officers were called to establish peace inside the building and out on the sidewalk.

Distraught and shocked people at the scene of a suicide, or any death for that matter, often acted out in violent ways, not only toward each other but toward the police. We tried our best to calm emotions while being on guard for a surprise attack from someone unable to cope with the shock.

The mother who tried to get my partner's gun out of his holster is one such example. If she had managed to get it out, what might she have done? Thankfully, we stopped her before anything happened.

CHAPTER 25

Suicide By Car Exhaust

I was patrolling an old-money neighborhood, three- and four-story homes, small lawns, and high-end cars. Just as I was fantasizing about living in one of them—complete with a maid, cook, and butler—dispatch punched through my daydreaming. She gave me the code for suicide and the address. I was just down the street from it.

The three-story house was pristine, as was the manicured lawn and other greenery. An ambulance sat in the driveway, and two EMTs and a woman stood next to it, her back to me. One of the ambulance crew walked over to me, flipping open a notepad. "The victim's wife is out of it with grief, so here is what I have."

Grateful that I wouldn't need to ask her the same questions, I copied his notes as he explained what they found. He said, "The husband is in that garage sitting in a Toyota. He ran a hose from his exhaust into his driver's side window. He died from carbon monoxide poisoning. I'll take you down there."

"Thanks," I said. "Give me a second to have a word with Mrs. Gladstone first."

I introduced myself and told her the EMT had given me the basic info. She managed to answer my questions about medications, if he had been depressed, if he threatened suicide in the past, if there had been marital problems, and more. There wasn't anything she told me that raised red flags that he might take his life. Time might change that and give her clarity. When I told her I needed to go to the garage, she said she couldn't look at him again. I told her I'd take an EMT with me and suggested she go into her house.

The old-style garage was prevalent throughout the neighborhood, narrow, low roof, shallow in depth. They were made for small cars built in the 1920s and 30s. The victim was behind the wheel, his head flopped back against the headrest. A garden hose ran from the exhaust pipe alongside the car and into the partially opened driver's window.

My suicide calls had been mostly hangings, firearms, and jumpers; this was my first experience with someone killing themself via carbon monoxide poisoning. I wondered what that must have been like for the poor man? Did he just sit there and take deep breaths, knowing full well that each inhalation brought him closer to that dark mystery? Did he fight his natural instincts to push open the car door, run out of the garage, and suck in the fresh morning air? Or did he even have time to think twice about his terrible decision?

Perhaps his intention was so all-consuming that he focused only on the goal until he lost consciousness. Or maybe he passed out before he had a second thought about what he was doing. No one would ever know the answer to these questions.

My sergeant came by and looked things over, and I ordered a van from the morgue. The last I saw of the deceased's wife was a slumped-shouldered woman moving slowly toward her house, arms folded, feet moving as if through deep snow. I waited 20 minutes until her sister arrived, then I went on to the next call.

I often wondered what was next for the survivors, especially those who lived in the same house where the death occurred. In this case, would the wife ever go into the garage again? Would she sell the house? Did the husband factor in that ending his life would also end the chance of it ever getting better? Or that his decision would assault his loved ones with physical and psychological pain?

After a murder, survivors usually direct their anger at the perpetrator. But when a death is by suicide, the victim is the perpetrator, the killer, if you will. So the survivor's emotions might be confusing and all over the place.

The person who dies by their own hand might seem to be a victim of mental illness or impossible conditions in their life. On the other hand, the survivor might perceive the suicide as a personal assault or dismissal. This can leave them feeling anger, rejection, and abandonment, intense emotions that are difficult or impossible to understand. Suicide can destroy everything the survivor took for granted about themself, their relationships, and their world.

How devastated and vulnerable the man's wife looked walking up to her front door.

Regarding this method of suicide:

The garden hose from the exhaust through the car window suicide method is well-known and often shown in movies, but it's less likely to work with modern cars. Not only is it possible to fail, but it will also cause extraordinary suffering during the process.

In the old days, carbon monoxide suicide could be done by simply running a car engine continuously in an enclosed space, like a garage, for a long time. Or by running a pipe or hose from the exhaust into the car.

Today, cars emit lower levels of carbon monoxide than days of old, that is, before the mid-1970s. Now when someone tries to kill themself in this manner of poisoning, it's not the quick and easy death depicted in the movies. People suffer a great deal.

First, they find it hard to breathe, then their thinking becomes clouded. The suicidal person will likely throw up and lose consciousness, which lowers the blood circulation rate. This, in turn, lengthens exposure to the gas and ultimately causes more damage to the body.

Depending on how long and intense the exposure, survivors can still incur long-term brain damage, such as profound memory loss and low brain function, and severe cardiac complications.

CHAPTER 26

Willamette River Drownings

The Willamette River divides the east side of Portland from the west, with 12 bridges available to traverse it—or jump from. The Columbia River divides Oregon from Washington, with two bridges. I rarely worked around the Columbia River and never had a suicide or accident drowning there. But I heard other patrol cars getting dispatched to drownings and occupied cars plunging into the river. The Glenn L. Jackson Bridge or I-205 Bridge that spans the Columbia has been the scene of accidents where occupied vehicles went off the bridge. In fact, the bridge had only just opened when a teenage driver bumped a second vehicle and sent a man, woman, and baby over the too-low-barrier wall and down into the mighty Columbia. It took days to find the three occupants.

The Willamette River doesn't have a sandy beach in Portland's core area but rather a sea wall, docks, and pilings. Instead of washing up on a shore, the waves bang the corpses into the sea wall or against pilings. Then as people enjoy a romantic evening stroll along the seawall, their moment is ruined by the sight of a dead person bobbing in the water.

How a found body looked depends on how long it was in the water. Some become caught in obstacles on the river bottom and stay down for long periods. If the body floating on the river bottom was free of entanglement, bacteria in the bowel and stomach produced gas, which usually caused the body to float to the surface. Body and water temperatures also affected the corpse's appearance, as did the presence of hungry fish and other water critters, and how calm or agitated the water was. One source said that bodies in sunken cars might look recognizable 30 years later.

The ones I experienced were bloated, their skin greenish.

One grey day

The dead man was lying on a dock on the west side of the Willamette River when I arrived at the scene. A boat crew had found him and moved him onto land before I got there. He was shirtless, shoeless, and the pockets of his trousers were turned out. His mouth was wide open, but I don't remember if he had eyes. Sometimes the fish ate them. If his were gone, maybe I blocked out the memory. Given the turned-out pockets and bare feet, I suspected a street robbery down by the seawall.

The medical Examiner got there and dropped to his knees to examine the man. His immediate guess was that he had been in the river for about three weeks. He checked this and that, as always, impressing me with how seemingly impassive medical examiners could be. One veteran ME told me that he was only affected when the deceased was a child.

As the kneeling ME did his thing, I stood a few feet away, talking with a second examiner. I mentioned the turned-out pockets and the possibility of a robbery. He had many more drowning victims than I and said it was common for the rapidly moving river water to do that to clothing. I told him the guy didn't have a wallet, but he assured me the water would take that too.

What face the dead man had left, I didn't recognize. I knew most of the regulars in skid row, but there were always "hobos" passing through. These were people, men mostly, who lived on the road— street-tough, often packing a club or big knife on the outside of their packs. Maybe the man on the dock had been one and crossed someone meaner. Or he could have been the victim of a hobo.

Or maybe the river robbed him of his possessions as it did his life.

I had looked away for a moment when someone over by the body cried out. I turned back to see small crabs, three of them, skittering out of the dead man's open mouth. They moved quickly in a line, over his bloated belly, dropped to the deck, and scampered surprisingly fast—toward me.

I like to think I didn't squeal, but I did move as fast as lightning out of their path. The little crustaceans kept moving in a straight row until all three dropped off the dock into the water.

I'm not a fan of water, that is, big bodies of water, so drowning calls always gave me the creeps. When I was a kid, a man saved me from drowning by reaching down into the water and pulling me to the surface by my hair. It's still a vivid memory.

My greatest phobia is to be submerged in a car. When I was writing my four-book fiction series, *Dukkha,* I wrote a lengthy scene in which four people in one SUV—antagonists and protagonists—punched through the seawall in San Francisco and sunk in the bay. I researched and interviewed people who had experienced such horror and survived. I also studied videos of submerging cars to see how the filling water made them roll and how the absence of light made it impossible to know which way was up.

I thought my research and writing the scene would toughen me up. It didn't. I still can't e watch it in the movies.

I've often wondered how many of those bodies pulled from the waterways were suicides, homicides, or accidents. Without obvious indicators—a suicide note left on a bridge, muddy slip marks on a river embankment, or evidence of homicidal violence—a body in a river, lake, or ocean is listed only as a "drowning."

CHAPTER 27

Almost a Suicide Drowning

We stopped about 20 feet short of the man so our marked police car wouldn't frighten him. Tom and I were both six-footers and 200 pounds; the jumper was taller and heavier. He was balanced on the riverside of the bridge railing, watching passing cars. When he saw us, he turned to look down at the churning waters of the Willamette.

The Burnside Bridge is arguably the most survivable of the 12 spanning the Willamette River unless the jumper drowns himself by purposely staying submerged. Since there wasn't anyone else on the bridge, the man clearly wasn't vying for attention, which is often the case. So my partner Tom and I wondered if he might be one to stay under until he drowned. Even if he were that type, many bridge jumpers quickly changed their suicidal minds when they penetrated the surface of those mighty rivers, the Columbia and the Willamette.

Whenever we approached dangerous people, we divided their attention by moving in from their right and left, specifically, their 3 and 9 o'clock.

A week earlier, we had used this technique on a mentally disturbed man cutting himself. We had been driving through skid row on a blistering hot afternoon when we saw him sitting with his back to a brick wall. His bare torso was drenched with sweat and covered with blood. It took us a second to register what he was doing.

He was gripping a large glass shard and was casually slicing long deep cuts from his face to his beltline, all the while mumbling gibberish. We radioed for an ambulance and got out.

He saw us but didn't stop with what he was doing. We spread out, Tom to the left and me to the right, and talked gently to him as we slowly approached, our moving palms extended. The extended palms, slightly circling, is a psychological trick that calms *some* agitated people; it didn't him. What did was our 3 and 9 o'clock approach as we took turns talking to keep his head turning right and left. When we were close enough, I took advantage of his attention on my partner, grabbed his blood-soaked arm, and forced him onto his belly. We got him handcuffed for his protection and ours just as the ambulance rolled up.

The jumper on the bridge didn't respond to our calming palm massage either. But our right/left approach kept the man occupied as we slowly inched in. At one point, we stopped and explained that we could help him and that we had lots of resources at our disposal. He wasn't buying it, but he was getting more agitated.

Tom said, "Ten-sixty-one," which was police code for "let's take him."

My partner kept talking without getting closer as I took mini-steps until I was within reach. As quick as a blink, he spun toward the river, let go of the railing, and began falling away from the bridge, his hands over his head.

Tom and I simultaneously draped across the railing and managed to grab his arms. The sudden weight drop crushed our chests into the steel railing and came close to tearing our arms from our shoulder sockets. If felt like it, anyway.

With the guy dangling in the air, his dead weight felt heavier than his 200-plus pounds as we struggled and groaned to drag him up and over the railing. He dropped to the bridge sidewalk, limp and weeping.

We transported him to a mental facility and never heard anything more about him. We thought about the guy over the next few days since our bruised ribs and aching arms were a constant reminder.

Cops prevent suicides every day. Whether they stop it from happening or show up afterward, they do their job, clear the call, and go on to the next one. There aren't medals given for preventing suicide and rarely does anyone ask the officer, "How are you doing" after they have been exposed to a particularly messy one.

Each officer is left to deal with it in their own way.

CHAPTER 28

Overdose: Brought Back From Death's Door

When I was a rookie, I spent two or three months in the Drug Unit working with undercover officers. While the drug problem in Vietnam was titanic, I was shocked that it had become nearly as bad in the US while I was gone. To my amazement, when I worked undercover, every time I asked a street person if they were selling, I either got a yes, or they said they knew where I could score. And these were so-called cold buys where the undercover officer walks up to someone in a park or a downtown street corner and asks, "You carryin'?" or, "You sellin'?" When I did it, the person always gave me an up and down appraisal, then a slight nod, and asked, "What you wanna buy, man?"

The few times I got made, they'd say, "Good evening, officer. I don't understand your question."

And it wasn't only street people who were involved. When tar heroin arrived in Portland, there were many ODs because users didn't know how to break it down to reduce its potency. We found one deceased well-dressed man in a Burger King sitting in a restroom stall, an expensive attaché case next to his feet, a hype needle still in his arm. The burger joint was on the edge of skid row, and the man was an attorney from one of the upscale law firms in the city's core area. He had probably used his lunch break to score some tar in skid row, went into Burger King, and injected the stuff that a minute or two later blew his heart apart.

Some readers might argue that the following story shouldn't be in this book's suicide section. I say a person who spends every waking moment looking to score "some good shit" is flirting with ending his own life.

Here is the story.

During my three-month tour as a rookie in skid row and 15years later, when I returned to patrol there for a few years, the major problem was alcoholism. The drinkers were called winos, people who spent their day inebriated, looking to score another bottle, and sleeping wherever they collapsed. It was typical that winos, even when completely sober, had a blood-alcohol rating that would make them legally drunk if they were behind the wheel of a car.

Around 1985, the area saw a dramatic increase in illegal narcotics users. Cocaine, of course, was popular, but the most sought after was cheap forms of heroin. The word on the street—"the word" was sometimes true, other times rumor—was that some dealers broke heroin down with Borax soap. Why? Because they aren't nice people. There was always bad dope coming into town, but knowing it was dangerous didn't stop the junkies.

People went looking for a high and found death.

Back to skid row. One day, my partner and I were parked at a corner in the heart of skid row, watching passersby and sipping coffee. As usual, the sidewalks were jammed with drunks staggering by and people looking to score drugs. We noticed a man standing out in front of Chief's Tavern, no more than 50 feet from where we were parked, saying something to each person who passed. His movements were quick and jerky as he no doubt asked, "You sellin', brother?" He desperately needed to feed his nose or arm.

Ten minutes later, a young woman stopped in front of him. They both looked around before shaking hands, the classic exchange of dope and money. Some days you could see it happening no matter what direction you looked. There were only so many cops and a lot more dopers. The seller, in this case, went south down the sidewalk, and the hungry buyer dashed into Chief's Tavern. We decided to get him before he consumed his purchase.

Just as we got out of the car, two inebriants began fighting by our trunk. We broke them up and shooed one guy east at the intersection and the other west. Then we proceeded to Chief's. We were almost to the door when the bartender rushed out onto the sidewalk and waved for us to hurry.

"What's going on, Kathy?" I asked.

"A guy's laying in the restroom. Looks like he's dead."

We zigzagged our way through the packed drunks to find two men standing over a pair of legs extending out from the restroom, the rest of the body was behind the partially open door.

My partner pushed it open. There he was. Less than five minutes ago, he was out on the sidewalk trying to score. When he did, it appeared he rushed into the restroom, shot up his purchase, and within seconds, the drug slammed a one-two punch into his heart.

I started to tell dispatch on my portable radio to send us an ambulance, but someone had already called them. I waved over the two EMTs coming through the door.

Within seconds, they were down on their knees on each side of him, one checking his neck for a pulse, the other retrieving a stethoscope. A moment later, both agreed that his heartbeat was weak and getting weaker.

I told them we had just seen the guy score dope outside, and he had most likely shot it up before we could get to him.

"We figured something like that," one of the paramedics said, nodding toward a hype needle on the floor by the doper's feet.

The other paramedic retrieved Narcan from his bag. According to medilibrary.org, it's "a powerful antagonist that antagonizes opioid effects by competing for the same receptor sites." In short, it reverses the effects of opioids.

I no longer remember if they gave him a shot or used the nasal spray, but within seconds the doper was yanked back from death and trying to sit up. The paramedics insisted that they take him to ER, but the man flatly refused. My partner and I pleaded with him to go, explaining that while he was alive now, he might not be later.

He stumbled to his feet and flung off our hands when we tried to hold him. Since we couldn't compel someone to go to the hospital, the ambulance crew left without even a thank you from the guy who, moments earlier, was being welcomed by the grim reaper. And of course, he wouldn't even give us a tip of his hat.

By the time we got back to our car, the man was again on the sidewalk outside of Chief's, asking passersby if they were selling. The Narcan not only brought him back to life, but it also negated the effects of the illegal drugs he had injected that nearly killed him.

The man still needed a fix.

I'm glad my early training tour through the Drugs and Vice Division was only a few months. I didn't like that world—at all. I didn't like looking scruffy and slouching around like a doper, and I didn't like communicating with people who seemed brain dead in their early 20s.

Every so often, bad drugs came into town and killed a bunch of people. I remember the first time when China White, a very pure form of heroin imported from China, made a fatal appearance. Street people were scared to death that they would unknowingly buy it instead of regular heroin. Being afraid of a drug is a good thing because it makes users more suspect when purchasing junk to shoot into their veins. Sadly, before word got out that China White was on the street, many people had already checked into the morgue.

One night, we served a search warrant on a woman who worked as a hair and makeup person for the movies. Portland has a very diverse look, so Hollywood likes to film in the city, giving many people work.

We searched all the usual places and were about to give up when we found blotter acid in the woman's refrigerator. Liquid acid, like "purple haze" at the time, was dropped onto sugar cubes for later consumption. Sometimes onto toast. Blotter acid drops were placed on perforated sheets of notebook paper, often in several rows. The drops were a half-inch or so in diameter. The doper could simply tear off one and enjoy.

The narcotic officers had the paper analyzed to make sure the drops were indeed LSD. What they learned shocked everyone.

The laboratory said the LSD had been laced with something else (if I heard what it was, I no longer remember), making the drops *extremely* deadly. So what is the difference between just deadly and "extremely deadly?" The lab reported that if a single drop was quartered and four people took only one-quarter, all four would die. (A narcotics officer friend disputed that could happen, but it's what we were told at the time by the lab people.) Either way, it's always a risk.

The drug world has always been foreign to me, though I was around it for all my years in law enforcement. I've never comprehended how some people live in that culture 24/7.

For example, I found it profoundly sad and ridiculous when a supply of bad dope came to town, resulting in a shock wave in the user community. I'd ask dopers, "Have you considered not taking drugs at all? That way, when bad dope comes to town, you wouldn't have a worry. See how it works? If you don't use drugs, you won't OD."

Yes, that was a little condescending, but some of them had already burned out a massive amount of brain cells, so it was essential to speak simplistically to be understood.

Incredibly, most looked at me puzzled, as if the concept to them was like "that's so far out, dude," to be considered.

When my kids were five or six years old and would run into the house with their knees and shins bleeding from falling on concrete, I'd say, "You were running up the cement stairs, right? You've been told not to, right?" When they nodded guiltily, I'd turn both palms up. I'd sink my left a little and say, "You run up the cement stairs, fall, and skin your legs." I'd hold my right palm in place. "You carefully walk up the cement stairs, and you don't fall and get skinned. Which one do you choose?" Of course, they'd choose the right.

If I'd asked dopers in this fashion about using or not using drugs, they would have pondered, then chose the left hand since, in their mind, the drug trip was worth the risk. Those who chose the right hand, and there would be only a few, were liars.

Some corpses laid out in the morgue like cords of wood looked like they had been at it a while. Sadly, the last time they chose the left hand, their hearts said, "enough already."

The healthy-looking dead ones learned the hard way, early.

SECTION THREE

ACCIDENTAL DEATHS

Depending on the study, the number one cause of accidental death in the US is either car crashes or poisoning. The latter is often ranked at the top because it includes overdoses.

The other common causes are falling, firearms, fires, drowning, workplace mistakes, and choking. Death by accidentally shooting (self or others) fluctuates between number 3 and number 8, depending on the list. One list noted death by suffocating, while other lists didn't include it at all. All those I found were compiled by reputable organizations, albeit not in complete agreement.

So many accidental deaths I went to were preventable. One of my early accident calls was the result of a man working on his car from underneath. He had placed the jack on a wobbly block that made the support precarious at best. When the mechanic scooted underneath his car, he discovered the nuts and bolts had tightened over the years. The only way to get them to move was to use force, hard yanks with a big wrench, which jolted the car on the feeble support.

Each forceful turn of the tool caused the jack to tilt more and more until it slipped off the block. The falling car crushed the man's head.

There are tons of videos on YouTube that depict accidents and close calls, many, sometimes all, are preventable. Of course, a boulder rolling down a hill, a collapsing bridge, a falling tree, and a lightning strike—are the result of being in the wrong place at the wrong time.

But so many accidental deaths are about poor decision-making or none.

CHAPTER 29

Saigon, Vietnam
Fatal Traffic Accidents

I quickly discovered that there were thousands of traffic accidents per day in war-torn Saigon. As I write this now, traffic accidents and fatalities remain one of Saigon's, er, Ho Chi Minh City's, top problems (it's still Saigon to me).

Although my current research found the reporting of traffic accidents, injuries, and deaths to be inconsistent, it's safe to say the numbers in all three categories are in the thousands. Judging by YouTube clips that show modern Saigon, it doesn't look like traffic has improved since I did daily battle in it during the war. However, there are no longer large military convoys charging through the city belching black exhaust into the air and into the lungs of anyone daring to breathe.

Here are three fatal accidents I came across in my first weeks and one I thankfully didn't see.

ARVN Through The Windshield

I had been in Saigon for about three days and had yet to be assigned a job. So I sat on sandbags outside of our quarters, watching the absolute insanity that was traffic. Imagine millions of motorbikes, pedal cabs, army convoys, French taxis, and bicycles, all moving with total disregard to traffic laws of which there were few. Well, it was worse than anything you could conjure.

On my first night, I saw a fatal; within 48 hours, I saw a dozen crashes, many of the participants injured.

There was a vast intersection directly in front of where I sat. To my left, a few feet down a side street, rock music poured out of a bar, the place packed with soldiers and prostitutes. Ten feet to my right, a military policeman sat inside a thick-cement kiosk hunched over an M-60 machine gun.

Six streets fed into the intersection. By the time the light turned green for one direction, a thousand vehicles had turned the half dozen lanes into a dozen more, all jockeying to be first off the blocks. I was mesmerized by the volume of near-misses I saw every five minutes or less, overwhelmed by the sound and fury of so many motorized combatants. When other MPs came up to introduce themselves, I had to read their lips because I couldn't hear a word they said, though they shouted next to my ears.

There was a sudden quieting, or maybe my ears selected the loud and long screech of tires out of the pandemonium. Whatever the reason, I jerked my head toward the oncoming lane directly across from me, just as a yellow and blue cab head-on crashed into another vehicle.

An ARVN soldier, riding in the front passenger seat, catapulted through the windshield, over the hood, and onto the pavement, landing like a sack of rags. Within minutes, his body was whisked away. Soon, thousands of vehicles continued their exhaust-belching trek, each set of tires tracking the blood away until there was nothing left but dry pavement.

The man was alive a few seconds earlier, then gone in the time it takes to face plant through a windshield's glass shards, fly through the air to splat spine and skull on hard asphalt.

It was the first time I saw a person's existence disappear <snaps fingers> just like that.

And life resume minutes later.

Fatal Bicycle Accident

While patrolling, we came upon a truck vs. motorbike, a daily occurrence in the teaming streets of Saigon. All that was left of the motorbike was a ball of twisted metal and warped plastic laying in a massive pool of blood underneath a truck.

We were told the motorbike's driver, a teenage schoolgirl, had already been taken away to wherever they put the day's traffic fatalities.

When I patrolled the day shift, we'd see scores of girls walking to school in giggling groups, all wearing their beautiful white *ao dai* (long dresses), their books clutched to their chests. Those who lived far from school buzzed by on their Hondas, their long black hair blowing behind them. Some shyly smiled at us, and I would say something to them in Vietnamese that always got a big smile in return.

Was the schoolgirl killed dodging her way through the crush of traffic as a million other riders did that same morning and every other one? Or had the large military truck been bullying its way through traffic, its deafening horn blaring, its driver bellowing out the window for people to move aside?

This was another early introduction to the terrible waste that were traffic fatalities.

Mamasan And A Sheet Of Cardboard

In the last story, "Fatal Bicycle Accident," the crash was between a Vietnamese citizen and a Vietnamese vehicle. Since it didn't involve Americans, it wasn't in our jurisdiction to act. When an accident involved American servicemen, the MPs had to investigate, a task that could take hours.

Six months into my year-long tour, I got my first day off (I still think Uncle Sam owes me overtime money.) My regular partner, Adam, teamed up with another MP. When I saw him later that night, he was looking pale and slump-shouldered. I asked how his shift went.

Adam said he and his partner were patrolling and came upon a small crowd of Vietnamese gathered along the side of the street watching a wailing mamasan. Some had turned their eyes away from what she was doing.

About 45 minutes earlier, an Australian military vehicle had driven down the street just as a little girl ran out in front of them. The horrific impact spilled the child's brains across the pavement.

Since the American MPs weren't there right after it happened and it's unknown if the Australian driver notified his superiors, some of what followed is left to speculation. For example, it's possible that Vietnamese police or Vietnamese MPs were on the scene and allowed the mamasan and the Australians to negotiate a deal. Likewise, Australian brass could have been called and was okay with a negotiated agreement. What is known for sure is that the Australian paid the mamasan off. I don't remember the amount, other than it was shocking low.

When Adam and his partner arrived after the Australian's had left, they were horrified to see the mother scraping her child's brains off the pavement with a piece of cardboard.

I've often heard people say that Vietnamese don't value life the same way we do. How stupid!

Of course, they value life. Theirs is an incredibly resilient culture that endured and survived hell not only for the 10 years we were there but also the decades prior. They fought daily for their survival, their loved ones, their children, and their friends. Sometimes they were successful; other times, they weren't. They starved, thirsted, and cried at the cruelty that weighted them down day and night.

Quite frankly, I seriously doubt that many in our privileged, overweight culture could have done the same.

Papa-San And The Ammo Truck

We were working combined patrol—MP Jeep, ARVN (South Vietnamese Army) MP Jeep, and a Vietnamese civilian police Jeep—following the civilian cops to a fatal accident about a mile from the front gate to Tan Son Nhut Airbase. Motorbikes, pedicabs, motorized pedicabs, bicycles, and military vehicles of every description jockeyed for space within the lanes, on the shoulders, and on the sidewalks. As we neared the accident, traffic came to a halt, but not the blaring horns and gunning engines.

Several weeks earlier, we were going nowhere quick in the middle of a traffic jam of epic proportions. If the heat and choking exhaust weren't enough, a monstrous ARVN truck was just inches from our rear bumper, the impatient driver leaning on a horn modified so people in Hanoi could hear it. My already cranky partner shouted several times at him to knock it off. Still, the ARVN continued with the 30-second blasts. When he increased them to 60 seconds, my nerve-frazzled partner climbed into our backseat and, like a crazed chimp, sprang onto the ARVN truck's front bumper, lifted the hood, and ripped out the horn wires.

Fortunately for the driver, he remained behind the wheel.

Now we were in another traffic jam, one caused by a fatality. Finally, there was a small opening, and the Vietnamese police jeep to our front quickly bullied us through, and we again began making headway.

A crowd had gathered around the accident scene. A large flatbed truck sat catawampus on the street, a motorbike beneath it wadded into a jagged ball. There had to be a bike driver somewhere, but I couldn't see him from where I stood. I pushed further through the crowd and… there he was, behind the rear tires, a man, or rather, what used to be one.

I'd seen a few dead bodies at this point in my tour, but I had never seen one completely flattened. My first thought was of the cartoons I watched as a kid where Bugs or Goofy got ran over by a steamroller. Usually, Elmer Fudd or Donald Duck would raise the flattened character like lifting a sheet of paper off the street, and *boing!* the squashed one snapped back into its standard rounded cartoon shape. That wasn't going to happen here.

One of the ARVN MPs knelt by the flattened man and scanned him from head to toe. His investigation complete, he turned to me and, with a grim expression, sliced his fingers across his throat. *"Fini,"* he said, using the French word for "finished." The man had an eye for the obvious.

It was then I noticed what the military flatbed truck was carrying, ammunition. At least a couple hundred boxes of it.

One time, I was standing in the wrong place at the wrong time and got picked to help unload a similar truck. The boxes weren't large, 12 X 15 or so, but they were pop-the-veins-out-of-the-neck-heavy.

Poor old papa-san got ran over by the truck's front tires and the rear.

Fini for sure.

––––––––––––

I saw many dead bodies during my Vietnam tour, and I would see more during my career as a police officer in Portland, Oregon. Most of them I have forgotten. A few remain in my head because of the circumstances or the grotesqueness of their death.

Such was the case with a traffic accident in Saigon that involved an American civilian, his chest crushed against the steering wheel and his leg jammed in a mass of warped metal. It took a long time to free his limb, and when we finally got it, his foot spun like a propeller on his shattered ankle.

Such terrible visuals never fade.

The sight and smell of these events forced me to ponder how the slenderest of threads connect life and death. I didn't understand the deeper meaning of this then (and I'm not sure I fully understand it now), but I swore to myself I wouldn't waste the life I had been given.

I like a quote attributed to many people, one of them Buddha, "The trouble is, you think you have time."

The above traffic accidents in Vietnam and many others "toughened" me a little to those I'd experience on the Portland Police Bureau. As I've mentioned elsewhere, sometimes the messier the death, the more it seemed unreal. A human isn't supposed to look like that mess lying there. So my brain would make it a mutilated mannequin or a Hollywood gorefest. That would last a short while, then my head would return to ugly reality.

Let's stay in Saigon for one more story not related to the terrible traffic.

CHAPTER 30

Saigon, Vietnam
A Swimming Pool Drowning

I had been in Vietnam about nine months when the brass decided to have a little party for the MPs. Someone had arranged for us to use a city swimming pool for an evening, people got a load of beer, and the mess hall provided all the fixings for hamburgers. I rarely got a day off from the 12- to 14-hour shifts, so I was looking forward to a few hours of mellowing.

It was impossible to see the pool from the street because it was surrounded by high walls, though the top portion of a 30-foot diving board was visible. Two years earlier, an American soldier was poised to dive when his head exploded, and his dead body toppled into the pool. Given that the area was always noisily congested with traffic and people, no one heard the sniper's round let alone knew from which direction it came.

Our party started well after dark. The pool area was lit poorly by one lone light bulb attached to a wall, but the fifty of us didn't care about the poor visibility; we thought we were in hog heaven. A couple of the guys brought bar girls, but no one paid attention to them as we were all busy chugging Budweiser, chomping burgers, and teasing one another. I looked up at the high board more than once and thought how terrible that must have been for everyone involved. Others thought the same thing because no one dived from it.

We had to get up at 0-dark-30, as they say in the Army, so we headed back to our billet before the 1 o'clock curfew, happy with beer buzzes and bellies full of burgers.

The following day, the duty sergeant assigned my partner and me to patrol the district that included the city pool. Around mid-morning, dispatch sent us there regarding a found dead body. I had never been there before the party, and now I was going for the second time in two days, albeit for two entirely different situations.

The body had to be American, or dispatch would have sent the Vietnamese police. All the MPs who attended the party had returned to our unit the night before.

An elderly Vietnamese handyman met us at the gate. As we followed him in, he explained that he saw someone lying at the bottom when he came in to clean. "American *chet* [dead] for sure," he said, pointing as we rounded the corner to the pool.

The dead man was lying where we had sat the night before, our feet dangling in the water. In his twenties, he was a thickly built man, wearing cut-off fatigue pants and an Army green T-shirt. There were no visible signs of foul play. We notified our sergeant, and procedures were set into motion to have the body picked up.

It was strange to think that someone, a GI or an American civilian, had died in the same place where we had relaxed just hours earlier.

Things were about to get a lot stranger.

We would learn in subsequent days that the medical examiners had determined the time of death to be before our party, not after. He had to have entered the pool after it closed to the public and before it reopened for the MP party; it was the only time the place was unattended.

It turned out the man was a soldier assigned to a clerical unit, not related to the MPs. He had apparently snuck in and had been swimming by himself when he drowned. Because a single light bulb poorly lit the pool area, we couldn't see the bottom.

As we splashed and romped like little children, not one of us knew a dead man lay beneath us on the floor of the pool.

Cold reality was never far away in Vietnam and always willing to insert itself at precisely the wrong time. The swimming pool party would have been a satisfying memory, but the terrible add-on tainted it.

In the early months of my tour, it seemed that a harsh reality followed every pleasant moment. It was as if Ares, the Greek god of war, knew we were enjoying ourselves, and he didn't like it. A found explosive device inevitably followed a few laughs with buddies at chow. If we pulled to the curb to talk with children, we were drowned out by a thumping Chinook chopper lumbering by overhead towing a shot-up smaller helicopter where men no doubt perished. A stop by the Saigon River to meditate on the rising sun would be interrupted by the rattle of an automatic weapon somewhere in the surrounding streets.

At first, I didn't find the transition from peace to ugliness to be an easy one. But after a while, I grew to accept the reality of it and to push myself to get the most out of each moment. If it was a good one, like a big thanks from a GI we helped or an enthusiastic wave from an old woman, I endeavored to enjoy it. If it was a bad moment, a violent bar fight or shots fired into a group of soldiers, I did my police job to the best of my ability and learned from the experience.

CHAPTER 31

Portland
A Traffic Accident With Multiple Fatalities

The street was and still is a busy one through one of Portland's industrial areas. At the time of the accident, the speed limit had been lowered to reduce vehicle crash fatalities. It didn't help since the two single-car accidents that occurred a year apart were speeding far beyond the legal limit.

When the second accident happened, I was a trainee, spending a few months in the many precincts and specialty units to gain familiarity with the job and all parts of the city. I was working Criminalistics—learning about fingerprinting and photography at crime and accident scenes.

My training coach and I were ordered to go to the morgue and collect hair samples from several dead bodies—one of them decapitated. We were told there had been a horrific high-speed accident on the industrial area highway. A rollover spilled a half dozen occupants onto the street, some of them killed. It was unknown which of the six was driving, though a clump of hair on the steering wheel would be the gruesome evidence to answer that question.

My coach explained that another speeding car with six occupants flipped and rolled in the exact location a year earlier. Some lost their lives in that one too.

We entered a room at the morgue where those killed in the accident lay on chrome gurneys. My coach took the hair samples, telling me to watch and learn. That was fine with me. I watched, but I also snuck peeks around the room as it was my first time there. There would be many, many other visits.

It was cold and semi-dark, with each victim's clothing folded neatly underneath their gurneys. Unrelated to our accident, one man lay under a sheet, his bloody jeans, a black and also bloody leather motorcycle jacket, and black boots packed neatly under the gurney.

When my young son became interested in motorcycles, I told him motorcyclists usually came in second place when competing with other vehicles for the same space on the road. This was true even when the motorcycle driver was legally in the right. I went on to tell him in bloody detail about a few of the accidents I had covered. He quickly changed his mind. (That technique probably isn't in a *How To Be a Good Parent* book, but it accomplished what I wanted.)

I looked back at my coach as he continued to collect hair samples from the deceased and place each one in a plastic evidence bag. It was a gruesome task in the chilly, semi-dark room, the air rich with the stench of fresh blood, and needless death.

I was transferred to another training assignment shortly after this, so I never found out if the samples proved who was driving that night, but it's safe to assume they did. It was too late to charge the driver with vehicular homicide and too late for him to live with the knowledge that his stupid choices snuffed out the lives of his friends. His family would be told, and they would have to deal with it.

So many lives were affected by that accident. Not only the ones who perished that night and those injured but also their families and friends.

Add to this list the police who investigated the initial accident call, the EMTs who responded in multiple ambulances, and the firefighters who washed gore off the street. My role in the hair collection in the morgue was minor, but I still remember that dark, cold room with the deceased.

Someone said, "Leave the bad memories in the past where they belong."

Tell that to this cop.

An officer friend on the east coast was behind a car on a freeway when it abruptly veered out of its lane and slammed into a cement wall. The officer jumped out and ran up to it to find a young couple inside, shaken but not seriously injured. However, the head-on damaged their car to the extent they were jammed in. The officer told them he was going to his vehicle to get a crowbar. He had just popped the trunk when their car exploded into flames, completely engulfing it.

The couple's dying screams are forever in the officer's head.

Vietnam was a 10-year war. When veterans first meet, they usually ask, "When were you there?" Some with recurring memories will say, "Last night."

It can be the same for our first responders.

CHAPTER 32

One Drunk Driver. One Dead Family

One warm summer night, an officer took a fatal car accident on a street named Hollins in southwest Portland. Hollins was always busy, so people who lived in the residential area had to do a lot of waiting before they could exit from their sleepy street into the rush of traffic.

A family of four, mom, dad, and two kids, were riding in the family car, on the way to a friend's house. They were on Hollins; the other vehicle, its driver drunk out of his mind, blew through the stop sign from a residential street and struck the family car.

All four members of the family died; the drunk driver was unhurt.

I wasn't involved in the incident since I worked a different shift at the precinct, but I did see the officers who were there. They were traumatized as they were all married and had children. But the case would get worse.

Months later, the officers involved went to court to testify about what they saw at the horrific scene—the slain family members and the unhurt drunk driver. They were anxious to know that the man would receive a heavy sentence for cutting short four innocent lives.

It didn't happen. The judge gave the driver probation, not one day behind bars. The trauma the officers had been living with since the accident turned to anger; the locker room wasn't a pleasant place that night.

As author Paul Craig Roberts said, "Justice is no longer a concern of the justice system."

Most officers have found the following to be true: The drunk driver more times than not survives, while those riding with them, or innocent people struck by the drunk's car are hurt or killed.

I was at only one accident where the drunk driver perished. I backed up another officer who asked dispatch for help because, as he stated on the radio, "I got a real mess here."

The accident occurred on an overpass that spanned several sets of railroad tracks. At first blush, it appeared that the drunk driver was traveling at high speed, crossed the center line into the oncoming lane at the bridge's apex, struck a car head-on, creating an explosion of glass shards and crushed metal.

I'd been on the scene a few minutes when I happened to look down one of the approaches to the overpass and noticed something near the bottom next to the guardrail. It was midnight, and hard to see it clearly, so I headed down to check it out, a walk of about 150 feet. I found a four-foot by four-foot chunk of twisted metal. It looked like a giant had wadded it up like a typist would crumple a sheet of paper to shoot into a wastepaper basket. I wasn't sure what it was until I used my flashlight to illuminate into the wad. There, deep in the folds, was a door handle.

The high-velocity impact had torn the car door free, clumped it nearly into a ball, and chucked it 150 feet down the onramp. It turned out to be from the drunk driver's car.

The first officer on the scene covered the deceased driver's ejected mangled body. The man reeked of alcohol and a whiskey bottle was found near his body. A grey blanket covered all but his nice shoes. They were brown and nicely shined. I didn't lift the covering off his head because there was no reason.

The ME would subsequently find his blood alcohol level far exceeded the legal limit.

If I had to guess, based on his expensive-looking shoes, I'd say he was a businessman, no doubt wearing a high-end suit under the blanket and a nice tie. Maybe the tie was a gift from his wife or daughter. Perhaps he had had cocktails with a business client, or he was just an alcoholic who liked nice shoes. I would never know, nor did I care.

What I did know was he drank to the point it affected his driving. He either thought he wasn't that bad, or he didn't care because he decided to get behind the wheel of his car.

Fate wanted someone to die in the terrible accident; I was glad it took the drunk driver this time. All the first responders were too.

CHAPTER 33

A Fatal Motorcycle Crash

I had a motorcycle for a short while when I was about 18 years old, proving that a bike and immaturity are not a good mix. I dumped it twice that I can remember, though the number was probably higher than that. The last time was when a car pulled out in front of me. I swerved, went down on my side, and slid partway under the big Chrysler. Ouch, but at least I survived long enough to sell the motorcycle and never get on one again.

As I mentioned earlier, in most if not all motorcycle accidents I investigated, in which it was bike versus motor vehicle, the cyclist came in second place. I went to one in which, I would learn later, the rider was protesting the new helmet law that required all riders to wear one. What could possibly be the argument against this?

◇ I have another head at home I can use if I crush this one on the street.

◇ Brains are overrated.

◇ The founding fathers signed something that gives me the right not to wear a helmet.

◇ I'm a fantastic driver. I never crash.

Anyway, the protestor was riding alone and went down on the side of his head. That was bad enough, but then he slid for 30-plus feet, grinding his ear completely off.

The last I heard, he survived it, but now he goes "huh" a lot.

Dispatch sent me to cover another officer on a motorcycle into a light pole on one of the streets that led into the downtown core. It was below zero on a January day. The other officer got there first and was kneeling by the motorcycle driver when I pulled up. The man's crumpled bike was wrapped around the damaged pole a few feet away.

"An ambulance is on the way," Ken said by way of a greeting. The look on his face told me the man wouldn't need it. I knelt on the other side of the victim.

Traffic was light, and it was early morning on a holiday. It was hard to tell if speed was a factor because even going the speed limit could destroy a face when it met a steel light pole.

Then I heard the death rattle.

I looked up at Ken. "He's been making that sound since I got here five minutes before you." He looked back down at the man. "So young," he said, more to himself than to me.

I've heard the death rattle before, a wet sucking sound, like a kid makes with a straw when he gets to the bottom of the glass. But it doesn't stop; it just keeps going as it gets weaker and weaker.

As we knelt beside the man, our hands patting his shoulders, I thought how 20 minutes earlier, he had been rolling along, enjoying the airy freedom of his motorcycle that so many riders talk about. Then something happened. Excessive speed, glancing at his watch, or an evasive swerve when a car cut him off. Then the sudden and brief realization that he no longer had control of his bike and that a six-inch in diameter steel light pole was rushing toward him to end his life.

I saw sudden death happen in other ways. But when it was from a traffic accident, I always contemplated the terrible waste that, in most cases, need not have occurred at all.

CHAPTER 34

A Death in Tangled Seaweed

One morning, I was reading the paper before heading to the precinct for my shift. There was an awful story of a 60-year-old man falling into a hole on the Oregon Coast. He was walking on the wet beach when the sand abruptly collapsed, dropping him into a pit full of tangled seaweed, crabs, and seawater. I remember folding the paper, thinking how horrible that must have been. It never occurred to me that I would see the man in a few hours—parts of him, that is.

Dave and I hit the street and handled a few calls before dropping by the morgue to have coffee with Stan, a medical examiner and friend. We greeted the secretaries in the front office, poured ourselves coffee, and headed back into the cooler.

Stan was typing at his desk in the far corner of the biting-cold room. Three occupied and sheet-covered gurneys were parked side-by-side against one wall, probably waiting their turn to be processed by Stan and the other examiners. There were empty gurneys in the room, too—the day was still young—as well as processing tables and suspended work lights. Another wall consisted of chrome fronted drawers, the occupied ones containing bodies awaiting processing or picked up by a funeral home.

Stan greeted us warmly and asked how our day was going. Dave answered with his usual, "Crime is our business, and business is good." I waved my hand at the room and commented that he was going to earn his paycheck today.

Our friend sighed tiredly and said, "You got that right. And we just got a nasty one in this morning. You guys see the piece in the paper about the man who fell into a hole at the beach?" My partner shook his head; I said I had. "Follow me," Stan said, standing. "I've had a lot of drownings, but this is a first for me."

We had seen many bodies in the place, from natural deaths to horrifically damaged ones. But none of those had prepared us for this one.

The smell of the beach—sea air, brine, vegetation, and dampness—greeted us before we got all the way into the room. Even the sickest Hollywood movie director couldn't conjure what was spread out before us.

A mass of slimy, yellowish-green seaweed, some with bulbous heads the size of softballs, lay piled across a long chrome table, seawater dripping off it onto the floor. The pile was about three feet high and five feet long. I looked at Stan, puzzled. "Where's the body—?"

"Oh!" my partner breathed. "Oooh my God!"

He was pointing at the closest end of the pile to us. I didn't understand his reaction. Was he alerting on the creepy-looking seaweed with their round heads, or was there something else that—

A single eye "peered" out at me from deep inside the seaweed. For an instant, I imagined the entire display to be a gag, a sick joke. Occasionally, MEs employed dark humor, a survival technique that doctors, firemen, and cops use to help them deal with the horrors they experience. No, this was terribly real.

Because the tangle of seaweed was so dense, I couldn't see if the eye was in a face as it should have been or, by itself, somehow detached from the victim's face and caught in the mess.

I moved a little, enough to see a lone hand protruding from the center of the mass, the fingers curled into a claw. At the other end of the pile, I saw flesh, part of a leg, I thought.

"Is he in pieces?" I asked.

"Mostly," Stan said.

"What the hell?" my partner said, pointing at several crabs working their way out of the tangles.

"We've already collected a lot of them," the veteran ME said a little too conversationally, I thought, given the scenario. "They attacked the man. Ate some of him too."

As used to seeing dead bodies as we were, this was too much. Dave and I exchanged looks, and as the case with longtime partners, that was all the communication needed. We told Stan we would see him later, and we left.

Author Terry Pratchett wrote, "It's not morbid to talk about death. Most people don't worry about death, they worry about a bad death."

How horrible this man's passing and for those who loved him. I hoped in time that his survivors found a way to bury the way he died and remembered the man, his life.

CHAPTER 35

Riley

During my first few years on the PD, I worked the 4p.m. to midnight shift in the largest patrol beat in Southeast Portland. I responded nonstop to domestic fights, armed robberies, burglaries, street fights, and vandalism. I remember many times running Code 3 to a hot call eating a sandwich I brought from home. That's not good for digestion, by the way.

I especially liked summertime because there were lots of people out in their yards. I enjoyed stopping to talk to straight citizens about their gardens and lawns and to see if they had any complaints about their neighborhood. It was an excellent way to get information about the crooks in the area.

Cops called one part of the area "Squirrel Heights" because there were many dopers, paint sniffers, burglars, and widespread violence. However, there was one relatively quiet street consisting of long-time homeowners who took pride in their neighborhood. Still, there is always that one house...

It was a three-story home with a wrap-around porch and a sprawling yard dotted with towering maple trees. The owners took care of the place but still found time to have lots of domestic problems. I'd been there a few times to referee family fights between the husband and wife and issues with their teenage son. The kid was a serial burglar and doper, well known to the district cops. There was no doubt in my mind that he was destined to Oregon State Prison. I don't remember what the husband-and-wife fights were about other than they were always fueled with booze, lots of it.

The couple had a daughter, Riley, 11 years old and unblemished by the other three.

One afternoon, I was cruising by the house, watching for the mother, father, or son driving (they were all suspended for DUI). Riley was out in the yard waving for me to stop. She ran across the lawn, her ponytail flying behind her, and practically slammed into the side of my car. She laughed at that, stuck her head through the open window, and asked, "How are you?"

Given the girl's parents and criminal brother, I was shocked to find her to be all sunshine, giggles, and sharp as a tack. Her ear-to-ear smile was contagious, as was her barely contained joy. We talked about her day, she asked about mine (I told her I rescued some puppies and helped some old people buy groceries), and I asked about her plans for the summer. She said she was going to spend a weekend with her cousins in Idaho. "They have a creek where we swim and stuff," she said with palpable enthusiasm.

I got a radio call about then, and I told her we'd chat more later. Her smile was brighter than my roof lights.

Two days later, I saw her on the porch. She leaped down the steps and bound across the yard, waving the entire way. She was excited to show me a bird she had formed out of clay. She sat on the passenger seat as I pointed out all the bells and whistles inside the car. I turned on the overhead lights and burped the siren. She was thrilled by it all.

I asked about her family, and she talked about her parents' fighting and drinking. She asked if I had kids, and I told her my first one was on the way. She thought that was exciting. I switched the subject back to her and subtly worked up to asking her if she felt safe at home. She said she did.

Over the next few weeks, we chatted often. That summer, I grew fond of her; she was a refreshing joy, the antithesis of the usual muck I dealt with every day in Squirrel Heights. I think she saw me as an adult who cared about her thoughts, likes, dislikes, and what she wanted for her future. The other adults in her life fought, staggered, slurred, and fell down a lot. I doubt they got around to talking about such things with her.

So often on the job, I saw parents who seemed perfect in all areas but had kids who were violent, sadistic, criminal, and consumers of every kind of narcotic. They spent their entire young lives in and out of the Juvenile Justice system until they were old enough to go to the grownup's prison. Conversely, I found parents who were the worst example of humankind but had great children.

One day, Riley told me she was going to Idaho for the weekend, so she'd see me the following week. She told me she would miss me, and I said I'd miss her too.

A few days later, I cruised by her place, but I didn't see her, and I didn't see her the next day or the one after that. On the fourth day, her mother came out on the porch and waved for me to stop. She approached tentatively, no surprise since her relationship with the cops had never been positive. She braced her hands on the windowsill, bent down, but looked at her feet instead of at me.

"I know that you and Riley have a connection." Uh oh, I thought. She wants me to back off.

"You've done a great job with her," I said to the top of her head. I wanted to add: Despite you and your husband. But I didn't.

She thanked me, barely audible. Then she looked up at me, her eyes wet. "Riley drowned over there in Idaho. I thought you'd want to know."

All the air sucked out of me. I just looked at the woman, waiting for her to say, "Just kidding." But it never came.

I gripped the steering wheel and stared out the windshield at nothing. A hundred thoughts scrambled in my head; my emotions were all over the place. I don't know how much time passed, but I jumped when the mother hacked a wet cigarette cough. I collected myself, stretched across the seat, and pushed open the door. "Please, sit."

We talked for a while, both of us teary-eyed. I no longer remember the details of Riley's death, but I know it occurred in that swimming hole she was so looking forward to. Finally, the girl's mother thanked me for being her daughter's friend and headed back to the house.

I don't remember if I got called to the home to referee family fights again, but I assisted in arresting the brother on at least one occasion. I remember he was a paint sniffer, a popular activity in Squirrel Heights. The enthusiast would spray aerosol paint into a paper bag, place it over his head, and tightly close the opening so fresh air couldn't get in. It wasn't against the law, but it often made sniffers act out violently.

For the next few weeks, I thought about the randomness of death and its terrible lack of logic. Why did Riley die, a little girl full of life and promise, while the son, a burden to his parents and a threat to society, got to live? There are lots of philosophical and religious answers to that question. Some make a little sense, some are ridiculous.

Consider this tragedy that happened in Vietnam.

On April 4, 1975, a Lockheed C-5A Galaxy airplane, participating in Operation Babylift—a program that paired American caregivers with South Vietnamese orphans—crashed at Tan Son Nhut Air Base. The plane had just left Vietnam and was over the China Sea when locks on the rear loading ramp failed, blowing open the cargo door. The pilots headed back to the airbase where they crashed in a rice paddy, skidded for a quarter mile, went airborne for half a mile, and slammed into a dike, breaking into four pieces. The fuel caught fire, and the aircraft burned.

Of the 328 onboard, 155 perished, including 78 children.

I did a Google search asking why bad things happen to good people. There are lots of answers. Some readers might take solace in one or more of them.

None of them worked for me, which can be a bitter pill to swallow.

SECTION FOUR

NATURAL DEATHS

In Portland, officers didn't respond to a witnessed death, such as those in nursing homes, hospitals, and home care situations. Unwitnessed natural death, they did. Other law enforcement agencies might have different policies on this. At the scene of a death unwitnessed, our job was to look for evidence of foul play and note any prescription or illegal drugs. A sergeant always came and medical examiners or people from a funeral home.

If we did find something that might look suspicious, we would ask dispatch to send a detective team and someone from Criminalistics to take photos and fingerprints.

Portland has lots of multi-floored buildings for low-income seniors. Some are nice, and some are terrible. The nicer ones cost more—one charges $11,000 per month—while the low-end ones are considerably cheaper and of poor quality.

There were four rest homes within my downtown patrol beat, including one that stretched nearly two city blocks. It was routine to get calls every month, sometimes more on an unwitnessed death. Typically, the person had died in their apartments, and after they were a no-show for two or three meals, someone with a key would check on them and discover their death. That's when we were called. Some months I was sent so often I got the aforementioned "Death Car" moniker.

I like to think I always handled the calls with sensitivity and professionalism. However, I must admit I grew tired of so many dead bodies. Even when a few days passed when I didn't get a call on one, I knew it was just a matter of time whenever I drove past a rest home.

Many seniors liked to gather in the lobby dayroom to watch TV, chat, or just stare in space, probably reflecting on their long lives.

When I got a call on an unwitnessed passing, I had to walk through the lobby to get the counter person to take me to the room in question. Like every other time I'd walk through a group of people, I'd hear the unoriginal, "I didn't do it!" or "Take ol' Bill over there on the sofa. He's a shady SOB." There would always be a sweet-looking blue-haired woman who would smile and a confused man who would tell me General Patton was a friend of his.

There was usually one or two who knew why I was there. "You here to check on Betty? We haven't seen her since Tuesday."

That always dampened the mood of the others.

By the time I checked the deceased, noted medication information, and looked for anything suspicious, the medical examiner or funeral home would arrive to collect the body. We often left the room together, rode the elevator down, and got out on the main floor. Sometimes the same people were in the lobby as if waiting to see their friend or acquaintance leave for the last time. Some looked with eyes that communicated everything from sadness to a profound understanding that we would come for them someday. A few wouldn't look at all.

About half of my 25 years with the Portland Police Bureau, I had no sense of smell. One day I woke up, and it was gone. I could still taste food, which surprised everyone. Still, I couldn't smell even the most intense odors—like dead bodies not discovered for two weeks during a heatwave in July.

A few times, neighboring beat car officers would call me on the radio and ask for a favor. "Hey Loren, I'm on a natural," they always began, "and judging by the smell, the man's been dead a long time. I'll buy you a cup of coffee if you go in and have a look around."

I always did and was never bothered by the odor.

I saw naturals not long after they passed, others I saw days after. One time I was present as it happened.

I was at the courthouse, and I was told my case would take all day. I never liked spending an hour in court, let alone an entire day, but I had had two dead body calls that week, and I needed a break from the street.

I entered through a door that necessitated walking by counters where people paid traffic fines, parking tickets, filed for a marriage license, and other pieces of city and county business. There were chairs and long benches where people sat waiting for their number to be called.

For some reason, my eyes fell on an elderly woman sitting on a bench. She was wearing a dress and sat with her purse on her lap, her arms wrapped loosely around it. I started to look away when I noticed water splattering on the floor between her feet. Yellow water.

She slumped against a man sitting next to her, then tilted forward toward the floor. I was too far away to grab her, but fortunately, others were able to catch her. She was a heavy woman, so all they could do was control her fall to the floor.

Two EMTs happened to be in the room, and they quickly dropped to their knees and tended to her. A few minutes later, one of them looked up at me and shook his head.

What follows is a small fraction of the naturals I was sent to investigate while on patrol.

CHAPTER 36

An Odd Death

At one time, Portland, Oregon's skid row, was a 12-square block of rootin'-tootin,' hard drinkin,' fist fightin,' knife stabbing,' and gun shootin' hotbed of violence. One area study conducted while I worked there showed more violent crime in skid row than in Oakland and Seattle combined.

Indeed, death was a regular on skid row. It had been that way for decades before I patrolled the area with my training coach in 1973, and it was still that way in the 1980s when I worked with a partner in a car and on a walking beat.

Some days it was common to find a dozen streets with passed-out drunks on the sidewalks, lying halfway into the gutter, curled up on the sidewalk, or lying under blankets in doorways. On those days when we were busy answering radio calls, we couldn't get to the sleepers and scoot them along. Nor could we call for the detox van for the exceptionally drunk. When the police couldn't clear the sidewalks, the hard Oregon rain would do it for us in the spring, fall, and winter. Or the flesh-frying sun in the summer would force people off the sidewalk skillet. Once everyone was up and moving, it wasn't uncommon to find a dead person.

Many winos called the streets their home for many years. So when they died naturally or violently, we had a record of officers transporting them to the Detox Center a few times, or a hundred times, or to jail when they had broken the law. Other than that, we knew little about them. If their drinking buddies at the scene didn't know their family history, we wouldn't know who to contact to report their death.

Sometimes all we had was a street nickname, and if their friends didn't know their real one, the morgue would file the deceased as "John Doe" or "Jane Doe."

In the years I worked there, it was clear that only the cops cared about the skid row population. The city council certainly didn't, nor did the businesspeople in the core area of Portland. As long as inebriates stayed out of the center of downtown, the high-rise executives and store owners were pleased.

Of course, not every person who lived in skid row was an alcoholic, doper, or criminal. There were law-abiding non-drinkers too. These were people who couldn't afford a better neighborhood and were forced to live in rundown flophouses that had been in deplorable condition since World War II.

One day, I got a call on a guy found dead in a low-rent apartment house in skid row. I had seen him around, but he had never been a police problem. The 76-year-old appeared to have died in bed, an undisturbed blanket tucked neatly under his neck.

After looking over the room and not finding anything suspicious, the apartment manager and I pulled the blanket and sheet down to the foot of the bed to observe the condition of the man's body.

The deceased wore a white T-shirt on which there was a small circle of red over the left side of his chest. We pulled the shirt up to discover a perfectly round hole over his heart with minimal bleeding. It looked like a bullet hole to me, so I called for a detective team to investigate and a medical examiner to pick up the body.

Often, I had to sit with the dead for several hours because there was a rush of deaths on those nights, or the morgue was short of medical examiners. Happily, this time one was close and arrived before the detectives.

I pulled back the covers to show him the hole in the man's chest. "Looks like a twenty-two caliber to me," I said. The ME got down close and personal and examined the wound, including sticking an instrument into it to measure the depth. (Early in my career, I saw several medical examiners probe bullet holes with their bare fingers. This was before AIDS, I should add.)

"Nope, not a bullet," he announced, straightening to his full height. "The man blew his heart. A full-on, very powerful heart attack made the hole."

"That can happen?"

He rattled off some medical jargon, the gist of which was yes, but it was rare.

I no longer remember if the deceased was displaying the horror grimace, which was often the case. However, the hole in his heart, I recall vividly.

The poor man died alone in his tiny flophouse apartment, located deep in Portland's skid row, a place with a violent history dating back to the 1800s. Some readers might be familiar with Portland, Oregon's Shanghai Tunnels, as they are often featured in those paranormal TV programs investigating haunted locations.

In short, from the mid-19th century to the early 1940s, the tunnels connected basements of bars, flophouses, and hotels to the waterfront. They were used to transport goods from ships to businesses, provide a place for prostitutes to ply their trade, and an underground route to carry unconscious drunks, victims of a knockout blow to their skulls, to awaiting ships. When they awoke in the morning, they discovered they were suddenly part of the crew. Hence the term "shanghai."

Many people have reported hauntings in the tunnels—voices, laughter, spirits—for years. Paranormal investigators have also experienced spirit activity and captured EVPs, electronic voice phenomena in the tunnels.

The elderly man in my story lived above them.

CHAPTER 37

A Dead Baby In A Drawer

I got a call on a dead baby.

It was in a poor neighborhood frequented by dopers and street gangs. There was a dive motel a block away from the call that was used by prostitutes for 30 minutes per customer.

The address was a fourplex, each apartment with three steps leading up to the door. Considering the rest of the street, it wasn't a bad-looking structure. A young couple was sitting on the steps of an end apartment, each holding tightly to the other, crying. I parked and approached them.

I waited until they looked up at me, their faces wet with tears. I asked, "Where is…?"

The man, who I would learn was the father, barely whispered, "By the bed. In the drawer. She was gone when we got up this morning." They asked if they could stay on the steps. "Of course," I said before taking a deep breath for courage, then heading inside.

The one-room, two counting the bathroom, was clean and neat. There was a sofa, chair, dinette, and TV on one side of the room and a bed and dresser on the other. I moved slowly toward the four-drawer dresser. Diapers were stacked neatly atop it.

The second drawer was partially open, revealing a pink bundle. I gently pulled it open farther.

The parents had made a cozy bed for the baby with a soft, clean blue blanket. A few weeks old at the most, the little girl was appropriately wrapped for the night, exposing only her head, her face blue.

Given the neatness and cleanliness of the apartment and the parents' appearance that didn't indicate druggies, my first thought was the child had died from SIDS, Sudden Infant Death Syndrome.

I went back outside and got the parent's and the child's information. They told me about their routine the night before, which included putting the baby to bed. They said they couldn't afford a crib yet, and not much of anything else for that matter. They were new to Portland and had just enough money to rent the apartment.

The detectives arrived, checked the baby, and talked with the parents. There were no new revelations, and they agreed with my thoughts. The medical examiner would determine the cause for sure.

When the detectives left, I sat out on the steps with the parents and waited for the ME to retrieve the body. I didn't speak. They cried.

The medical examiner came within the hour, and I left. I really needed a breather to process what I just experienced, but we were shorthanded, and all cars were running from call to call. As soon as I cleared the deceased baby call, dispatch gave me a theft in an affluent neighborhood at the far end of my beat.

The complainant met me in the yard, and before he uttered a word, I could see he was angry. "You know how long I've been waiting?" he bellowed. "I pay taxes for police service. And I pay your salary."

Often when people would tell me this unoriginal claim, I'd say, "Really? You pay my salary? Can I have a raise then?" But he was already steamed, so I bit my tongue. I tried to apologize to him, but he didn't want to hear it. He wanted to vent. So I let him for about a minute, but then he began to insult me personally.

Considering how I was feeling after the dead baby call, my patience was short with his kind. I turned around without saying a word and headed for my car. He shouted, asking where I thought I was going. I turned and said simply, "I refuse to take your report." With that, I got in the vehicle and left. I told dispatch that I was refusing the call because the man was belligerent.

I never heard anything more about the incident.

I did hear about the baby. It was SIDS.

Children's doctor, Dr. Burton Grebin, said, "The death of a child is the single most traumatic event in medicine. To lose a child is to lose a piece of yourself."

Officers know this all too well, whether it's at the scene of a fatal traffic accident, drowning, a natural death, gangbanger drive-by shooting, or any other type of fatality. Most cops sign on to protect people. Period. Though the child's death isn't their fault, they feel it all the way to their bone marrow.

The image of that precious bundle lying in the dresser drawer, so still, so blue, remains.

For further information about SIDS, go to the website, Mayoclinic.org, and type "SIDS" into their "Search Mayo Clinic" box.

CHAPTER 38

A Dead Man On An Icy Hill

It was a bitterly cold winter day, and I was working alone downtown. The streets were treacherous as it had ice-rained the night before. It takes two seconds to dent a police car in icy weather but two hours to do the paperwork afterward. Since chains aren't much help on black ice, I decided to reduce my risk by parking at an intersection to watch street activity. As writer Robert Burns said, "The best-laid plans of mice and men…"

I had no sooner settled in than I got a radio call out of my regular beat to a dead body in one of the hilliest parts of the city. *"Be advised,"* dispatch said a couple of minutes later, in which time my tires had yet to find traction to pull away from the curb, *"The deceased is lying in the street."*

The location was 20 blocks away, and according to dispatch, the body was lying in the middle of Davis Street on 24th. Twenty-Third was the main street, and those numerically higher had a greater uphill slope. Why hadn't the body slid down to 23rd? I wondered as I worked my way there.

The five-minute drive took nearly 30 minutes. I parked on 23rd as there was no way I could drive up to where I could see the body in the street. There were half a dozen people standing on the sidewalk across from it huddled into their coats. Two of them looked like they might be EMTs.

Climbing the sidewalk slope reminded me of a saying we had in the Army when traversing through the mud: "Take one step forward, slide back three." On black ice, there was that and a lot of stopping my fall with my hands against the frozen cement.

Finally, I arrived. I looked down the sidewalk I had just traversed. If I were to slip, there were trees and bushes I could grab to stop my unwanted descent. However, in the middle of the street, I would just keep sliding all the way to 23rd, where a city truck dumping sand would run over me.

The EMT guys had approached from the top of the hill. Apparently, it was quite a show as they slid past the deceased then had a dickens of a time getting back up to him.

The poor man was in his 50s. His head was facing uphill, so maybe he had a fatal heart attack trying to get up to his home. I slid a few times walking around him looking for evidence of foul play. Once, I nearly grabbed his ankle when I slipped. Sliding all the way to 23rd, holding onto a dead man's foot doesn't make for good PR.

The ME arrived, and we had another challenge getting him onto a gurney and up the hill to the van.

Few people plan where they are going to breathe their last. As such, it's the first responder's task to move them from where they died to an ambulance or the ME's van. This can be a challenge on so many levels, some stomach-churning.

Early in my Vietnam tour, I helped carry an unconscious obese American civilian on a stretcher down two flights of stairs. He had rammed a bottle of Johnny Walker Black up his rectum for some unknown reason, making all aspects of our encounter unpleasant. I don't know if he survived.

First responders do their jobs not expecting thanks. It's a good thing because they rarely get it anyway.

CHAPTER 39

The Death Of A Clock-Loving Wealthy Man

Strong winds whipped sheets of rain across the street, sending garbage can lids and pieces of trees bouncing across the lanes, some of them smacking against the side of my patrol car. Just when I was looking for a place to pull over until the worst of it subsided, dispatch gave me a natural death. The call was in the patrol district next to mine. The beat officer was off to jail with a prisoner, so I got the honors. I would have preferred a theft call, but I'd take a DB just to get off the street for a while.

The tiny house was the only home on the street; the rest of the block consisted of lots overgrown with weeds where once a neighborhood had stood. A woman fighting an umbrella met me outside the place. She said she worked with the occupant, and since he had missed several days of work, the boss sent her to check on the man. She still had a key from when she watered his plants when he traveled abroad the previous spring.

Before I got there, she had unlocked the door, peeked in, and saw the deceased lying on a bed in the living room. It scared her, so she retreated and waited for me. I told her to wait in her car while I checked the place. If the death resulted from a crime, I didn't want the scene contaminated any further.

"I hate to say this," she said, relieved, "but the odor is horrible."

This wasn't a problem because I didn't have the sense of smell (explained earlier). I pushed open the door and peered into the dreary space. There were no lights on, and since the heavy sky and punishing rain darkened the outside world, it was even dimmer inside. I found a light switch on the wall just inside the door.

The room was small and cozy, with a hospital bed in one corner on which the deceased lay on his back. He was an enormous man, both in length and bulk.

I glanced around the room, noting pills on his dresser, clothes folded neatly on a chair, and a stack of books. On the wall above him were two beautiful cuckoo clocks. They looked to have been intricately carved from rich wood. I wondered if he had them on silent since, to my mind, coo-cooing every 60 minutes would not make for quality sleep.

I turned to look at the wall on the left. More clocks, a half dozen of them, all of them the cuckoo variety. Likewise, with the wall on the right, eight of them there, all high-end looking and artistically designed. But wait. The back wall displayed another half dozen.

They all showed a few minutes before the noon hour, some a little faster, some two or three minutes slower. Were the clocks all set to coo-coo audibly? I had been to the Tiki Room at Disneyland. In that fun place, dozens, maybe a hundred electronic birds rambunctiously sang and carried on. This place would almost be as insane.

I wanted to hurry up and get out of the house before the noon hour struck. I turned to head into the kitchen when I saw a stack of greenbacks on an end table next to an easy chair. It consisted of several banded, 20-dollar bills, at least a thousand dollars. There were more on the coffee table and on an old-fashioned dinette in the kitchen. I walked back into the living room and noted more banded stacks on a dresser top. The more I looked, the more I found stacks and stacks of banded bills. There had to be thousands and thousands of dollars.

If it hadn't been for the multitude of cuckoo clocks, I might have thought I was being set up. I had heard rumors that the department had on occasion set up cops with planted money to see if they were honest and take them to the Property Room. No one I knew on the PD had had it happen to them, but the rumor persisted. I did know that one of the local news stations sent a man into a precinct to turn in a "found" wallet with 20 dollars in it to test the desk officer's honesty. To the news reporters' chagrin, he placed it in the property room. The TV station's upper echelon got a stern reprimand from our chief for wasting the officer's time.

But in this case, given the multitude of clocks, it would be a safe bet that the deceased was a little eccentric.

Noon happened while I was still inside. The riot of coo-cooing clocks was a worse pandemonium than I anticipated. I rushed out onto the porch.

As the out-of-sync cacophony continued for five minutes, I called Criminalistics to take photos of the money, bag it, and place it in the Property Room.

Two days later, I saw a small article in *The Oregonian* newspaper about the man's passing and that there had been over $150,000 found in his home. The story said that authorities hadn't been able to locate a relative. If they were unable to find anyone, the money would be turned over to city coffers.

I'm often asked after telling that story if I were tempted. No, I wasn't. I did think a couple of times how great it would be to have a few bands of 20s, but my fantasy never went beyond that.

Everyone has a story; some keep theirs close, while others reveal theirs when you show that you're genuinely interested. I wish I had known the man before he died. He was probably a fascinating guy in a quirky kind of way. Was he captivated by the classic cuckoo-coo clocks, or was he preoccupied with time?

If it was the latter, his time ran out far too soon. He was only 40.

CHAPTER 40

Uncomfortable

I had just left dayshift roll call and getting into my patrol car when dispatch gave me a natural. What a way to wake up.

Two weeks earlier, my partner and I got a fight call right out of rollcall. The brawl was on the second-floor landing of a building, and we could see the men thrashing above us as we ran up the stairs. We were three steps from the top when the two of them fell onto the stairs and tumbled toward us. They hit us like two 200-pound bowling balls taking us down the stairs with them. We had nearly rolled to the bottom of the long staircase when I heard my partner, from somewhere in the pile of thrashing arms and legs, yell, "We haven't had coffee yet!"

Getting sent to a natural so early was about as bad.

It was in a pleasant bungalow in a well-kept neighborhood. I was greeted at the door by a 30-something woman in tears and invited in. The door opened to the living room. To the immediate right was a smaller room, probably meant to be an office or study. However, the owners of the home had made it a bedroom. The door was open, and I could see a pair of legs hanging over the end of a bed. The rest of the room was blocked from view by the door frame.

There were half a dozen other people in the living room, all looking solemn, some weeping. I nodded at everyone. The woman who let me in introduced herself as the deceased's granddaughter and gestured for me to follow her into the bedroom.

The dead man was lying back on a made bed, his lower legs draped over the edge, his slippered feet not quite reaching the floor. He appeared to be in his 80s, wearing a grey, one-piece jumpsuit.

The body's position looked like he had probably been sitting on the edge of the bed just before he died. Maybe he had been preparing for the day and had sat down to put on his slippers when his heart suddenly stopped. Or he had been doing whatever, when he began to feel not quite right, a little dizzy perhaps, and decided to sit down until the feeling passed. But it didn't, and he fell over backward, dead.

I asked the usual questions: Was he on medication? Had he been ill? Was he under a doctor's care?

Looking down at the deceased, the woman said, "You might know his son; he's a policeman." And she told me his name.

"I do know him," I said, and I named the division he worked in.

He was also my next-door neighbor. I had recently hired his carpentry skills to build a second-story deck on my house.

"He's on his way," his sister said.

I was not comfortable with this.

About a year earlier, we were informed at rollcall that an officer named Culpepper was involved in an accident off duty the day before, and his wife Sharon was killed. A few hours later, my partner and I were at the morgue on another matter. While the medical examiner was talking with us, I glanced over to the wall of drawers. Sharon Culpepper's name was written on a chalkboard next to one of them, with yesterday's date.

On another occasion, I saw another officer's wife's name on a mausoleum drawer. She had died after a long illness, we were told at rollcall a week earlier. The flowers attached to the drawer were fresh. Those on other drawers were old and crumbling.

I remember feeling intensely uncomfortable seeing Sharon Culpepper's drawer in the morgue and seeing the mausoleum drawer that held another officer's wife, both recently dead.

Why?

I didn't know them, but I did know the officers. Their wives' deaths were a profound event in their lives, and I felt I was intruding, almost as if I were peeking through a window into their home. The drawer in the mausoleum was in a public place, but the one in the morgue wasn't, at least not to the extent of the mausoleum drawer. Still, I saw it.

Seeing my neighbor's father was a different situation, but I knew the officer quite well. I didn't recall if I had ever seen his father at his son's house, but if I had, I'm not sure that would have changed my discomfort at seeing where he breathed his last.

Besides feeling that I was intruding on my neighbor's personal tragedy, he would know the job necessitated me to perform my role as the responding officer. I had to ask specific questions, survey the place for anything suspicious, take note of prescription drugs, make calls, and say nice things to the survivors. He would know I was doing all this while, at the same time, his sorrow was ripping his heart from his chest.

So I didn't want to be at the house when my neighbor showed up and found me there. But police procedure required that I not leave until the medical examiner got there to recover the body.

Typically, the ME seemed to take forever to arrive at a scene, as I've mentioned in other chapters. This time they were quick to come. I again apologized to the granddaughter for her loss, nodded to the gathered family, slipped out the front door, and speed-walked to my police car.

Is my take on this weird? Maybe. It's my quirk, and I'll admit to it.

About a year ago, as I write this, I saw the officer in the supermarket, looking quite feeble, out of sorts, and supporting himself with a cane. A younger woman, perhaps a granddaughter, was holding his arm. He was long retired, and we hadn't been neighbors for 30 years. I debated going over to say hi, thinking he probably wouldn't remember me. When I finally decided to do it, he and the woman had left.

He died a week later.

CHAPTER 41

A Bloody Natural

"Suspicious circumstances," dispatch said. So what did that mean? I wondered as I headed to the apartment building. A possible homicide? Suicide?

I met the apartment building manager in the parking lot. She was clearly in shock and squeezing her clenched hands in against her chest. "It's something awful," she managed. "Mister Burger was a lovely man. I can't imagine who would do something like this to him."

As we climbed the stairs, I asked how far she had gone into the apartment

"I pushed open the bedroom door," she said. "I didn't touch anything except for the door handle and light switch. The next apartment over, number twenty-seven, Ally said she heard some noises in the middle of the night, groaning and what sounded like thumping. Mister Burger lived alone."

I looked at her. "Thumping?"

"Ally said it sounded like thumping on the wall." She stopped and pointed at the apartment three doors down. "That one there is Mister Burger's place, number twenty-nine. I don't want to go in again." She handed me the key.

The living room was clean and neat. I headed toward the open door that had to be the bedroom in the small apartment, it's ceiling light on. I pushed the door open the rest of the way and stood there stunned.

Blood. Everywhere.

The man was on his knees, his head and shoulders jammed into a small space between the nightstand and bed. The lamp on the nightstand lay on its side, medicine bottles scattered around it. Blood dotted the wall behind the bed and on the pillows. The other walls dripped with red as if slopped on with a broad paintbrush. The carpet and bedspread were sopped.

It looked to me that there had been a violent and prolonged struggle, the victim and attacker bouncing off three walls and thrashing about on the floor.

I called for a detective team.

The detectives and medical examiner determined that there hadn't been a second party involved at all. The man's death was a natural. The ME explained that the man's agony, and no doubt fear, drove him to thrash all about the room vomiting copious amounts of blood.

Natural was the wrong word, I thought, considering how much pain he must have been in. "Horrifying," "horrendous," "dreadful," were all more apropos than natural.

This incident occurred before I lost my sense of smell. Due to the volume of blood in the room, it was an assault on my olfactory system. The stench was at once damp and copper-like. The latter because of the presence of minerals in the blood. There was the stench of vomit and feces, too. I could smell all of it. And taste it.

According to the National Institute of Deafness and other Communication Disorders (nidcd.nih.gov), "Your sense of smell is also influenced by something called the 'common chemical sense.' This sense involves thousands of nerve endings, especially on the moist surfaces of the eyes, nose, mouth, and throat. These nerve endings help you sense irritating substances-such as the tear-inducing power of an onion-or the refreshing coolness of menthol."

And massive amounts of blood, I might add.

The sight of the bedroom, the lasting visual in my head, was on a par with the worst homicide I had experienced. May the poor man rest in peace.

When it's our time, may we fall softly to sleep and
pass gently into death's warm embrace.

Loren W. Christensen

CHAPTER 42

Until Death Do Us Part

January midnight, and the wind and ice rain were making driving nerve-racking. It was the end of a very long shift, and I was heading back to the precinct, wondering if my private car could negotiate the worsening streets. Dispatch called my number. They were good about not giving officers a call so close to the end of their shift, so I assumed it was urgent. It was a dead body with suspicious circumstances. The address was a duplex.

An EMT and a man sucking hard on a cigarette stood on the porch talking. My car slid on the ice to the curb, and I cautiously walked toward them, ice pellets stinging my face.

"It's my girlfriend," the smoker said by way of a greeting. He was in his mid-20s, his face taught and pained, his hands trembling. "I don't know what hap…" He choked off a sob. "Sorry. She just suddenly wasn't moving."

I told the smoker to stay where he was and followed the EMT inside. The living area was just large enough for a sofa and TV. A pair of all-glass French doors on one wall separated the living room from the bedroom. The doors were open, revealing a naked young woman lying on her side across the bed among a scattering of pornographic pictures torn from a magazine. Another EMT was standing at the foot of the bed, writing something in a notebook. He looked up and nodded.

"Nothing out of the ordinary that we can see," he said. "No injection sites, no red or bruising around the neck, no red marks on the face from a punch or kicks, nothing."

I told him that a detective team was on the way. Dispatch had ordered one, assuming I'd want one given the circumstance related to them by the caller.

I went out onto the porch to talk to the boyfriend who was puffing on a fresh cigarette, the ice wind whisking the smoke away. I got his name and the victim's information. He said they had been boyfriend and girlfriend for the past two years.

"We were having sex," he said without embarrassment. He shook his head. "And she just…died." There were no tears, but not everyone reacted the same way. I asked about drugs, and he said they didn't use them. "Kam was healthy…at least I thought she was. She hadn't been sick or anything."

The detectives arrived a few minutes later. One interviewed the boyfriend while the other followed me in to look over the death site. I said I had given the area a cursory look and didn't find any sign of drugs or drug paraphernalia in the bedroom, kitchen, or bathroom.

Shortly after the EMTs left, the detectives released the boyfriend explaining they would inform him of the medical examiner's autopsy results. The detectives told me they had a shooting to go to and headed out into the storm.

Dispatch said the MEs had other bodies to pick up before they could get to me. They couldn't provide an ETA given the terrible weather and bad streets.

There wasn't a thing to read in the place, so I sat on the sofa listening to the clatter of ice rain against the window panes and the occasional wind gust. The dead woman, now covered with a blanket, lay on the bed about 15 feet away.

At one point, I got up to take another look for anything out of the ordinary. There was a dresser in the living room. The top three drawers contained underwear and T-shirts. The bottom one held jeans and a dinner plate with a partially eaten porkchop and a bite or two left of mash potatoes and peas. It looked like it had been in there for a few days. So that was weird.

I commented elsewhere that my presence at natural deaths always made me feel I was imposing on the victims' personal space and the emotions of friends and family. That might sound silly, but it's how I felt invading their home, going through some of their things, and eyeballing the deceased for foul play.

So what could be worse?

Investigating a naked young woman lying in a bed covered with porn pics who died while sharing intimacy with her boyfriend was the epitome of invading one's personal space. There wasn't one snicker or uttered black humor comment from the EMTs, detectives, or me. Everyone that night was professional and compassionate to the young man.

I've studied the paranormal for years and written fiction and non-fiction books on the subject. I must admit that waiting in that tiny apartment with a dead person as wind and ice rain rattled and trembled the old building was a tad disconcerting.

CHAPTER 43

Dead Man Against A Fence

I pulled to the curb where a dead body had been found along a fence that ran along I-405.

An ambulance was already there, its flashing lights the only color in the grey and bitter-cold February day.

The complainant, a street person, pointed down a 20-foot slope toward a seven-foot-high cyclone fence and equally tall raggedy bushes bordering another slope that descended to the freeway. "The dude's down there," the man said with a jerk of his thumb. "He's kinda in parts."

Two EMTs pushed their way out of the brush and headed up the slope. "Bad one," one of them said as they neared.

A small crowd had gathered across the street. I asked everyone to stay there while we investigated the scene. Two people from the Medical Examiner's office pulled up in a van. One was a man long past retirement and straight out of Hollywood casting. He looked a little like Slender Man, the fictional supernatural character that was a big thing on the Internet a few years ago that many kids thought to be authentic. Slender Man and the elderly ME were exceptionally tall, skinny as a bean, with pasty white skin that had never been exposed to the sun. Both wore a black suit way too short in the arms and legs.

His partner was a high-energy guy barely old enough to hold the job. He reminded me of a rambunctious puppy bounding about his father's feet. The three of us headed down the slope.

The deceased was lying flush with the fence, his clothing and most of his exposed skin rotted away. His head, which lay about five feet from his torso, was not much more than a skull with dirty white bone and some black hanging flesh. His clothes looked to be mission handouts given to street people by the Salvation Army. Yellow and dead weeds had sprung up between his sprawled legs and between his arms and torso.

We would learn that he had been lying between the tall bushes and fence for at least a year, probably longer. The street we were parked on saw light traffic, and the rare pedestrian would have to have gone down the slope and pushed through the foliage before finding the body.

The medical examiner Slender Man told the kid to go back to the van, get a body bag and gurney, roll it down the slope, and start loading the body. The assistant sprang away with all the enthusiasm of a 10-year-old being told he was going to Disneyland.

"Is it a man or woman?" I asked, looking at the body. "The clothes are for a male, but sometimes the Salvation Army gives folks what they have, regardless of male or female."

Slender Man shrugged. "We won't know until we get the body back to the office."

When I saw the kid coming down the slope with the gurney, I headed back up to the sidewalk before they asked me to help. I crossed the street to talk with the onlookers. It was a painfully cold winter day, so only the very morbidly curious remained to get a peek at the body.

We chatted for a minute or before a woman pointed behind me and shrieked, "Oh my God!"

Slender Man was carrying the head up the slope.

Two things I never got used to on the job. Arriving at a car accident to find one upside down was always a bit of a shocker. Year after year, we see vehicles going here and there on all their tires. To see one on its back, sometimes with a bloody arm draped out the window, always took a moment for me to wrap my head around. Motor vehicles just aren't supposed to be that way.

Likewise, heads should be where they were designed to be, on top of and between two shoulders. Seeing a head unattached didn't compute in my mind. It was an unacceptable horror.

When I was in the academy hearing stories from veteran instructors, I hoped I wouldn't have to deliver a baby in a dive hotel or at the scene of a horrific traffic accident. Mostly, I never wanted to see a decapitated head. As it would turn out, I never had to deliver a baby.

Slender Man held the skull—partially covered with black rotted tissue—between both his palms as he walked up to me. "You were asking me how to tell the gender of a decomposing body," he said, his tone that of a bored college professor. The skull's face was angled up, the hole where the neck used to be turned toward Slender Man. Out of the corner of my eye, I saw the small crowd moving toward us. "There are several ways," the ME lectured. "One is the thickness of the bone structure where this fella's eyes used to be."

With that, he tilted the skull, so the face was "looking" at me, the hole that used be the man's neck straight down. He extended it closer as he said, "Notice the sharp edges around the socket—"

The crowd gasped, and at least one person screamed as black sludge streamed out of the neck opening and splattered heavily at our feet. "Oh dear," Slender Man understated, "there seems to be…"

The rest of whatever he said was lost on me as I felt my stomach churn and my breakfast began to rise. Cold sweat broke out on my forehead in the frigid winter air.

I stepped away from the man and the terrible thing he brought up the slope to show-and-tell with me and, inadvertently, the crowd. I walked a few steps toward my police car. *Don't throw up in front of these people,* I thought. *Don't throw up in—*

I looked back; the onlookers had left anyway, the last of them hurrying around the corner at the end of the block.

Over by the van, Slender Man and his puppy were fussing with the body bag and gurney the young man had just wrestled up the slope. I could see the skull's "face" and part of a foot protruding from the unzipped bag as they appeared to be taking inventory. I was too far away to hear the veteran's words, but his tone sounded like an admonishment. The kid dipped his head with deference and scrambled back down the slope. I was halfway back when the kid burst out of the shrubs holding something up in the air.

"I found it!" he shouted. "I found the other hand!"

Slender Man was shaking his head as I walked up as if to say, "They're hiring idiots these days."

In subsequent days, it was discovered that the deceased had been homeless and not seen for over a year. The man's remains showed no evidence of foul play, and the decomposition was typical given how long the body had been exposed to the elements.

Of all the unpleasant sights I saw in my years on the PD and as a military policeman, that was the closest I came to "calling Ralph," as vomiting was called in the Army. I was amazed at how I instantly flushed sweaty hot from feet to head in the 30-some degree day. I even felt a little faint.

The sight of blood never bothered me, even lots of blood. The smell of it—the few years on the job when I had a sense of smell—I found unpleasant, but it never affected me as much as seeing the black goo pour from the skull.

I always tried to stay neutral and unaffected regardless of what was going around me. This time, I couldn't.

Cops are supposed to remain unemotional on the job, which sometimes upsets people. "Why aren't you upset that my child ran away?" one mother shouted at me when I was taking her report. Another person bellowed, "You just stand there with your blank face while I'm bleeding and swelling."

I never responded to such comments because I knew they were said in the heat of the moment. Some even apologized later for their verbal attack, saying they understood that officers had to keep their emotions in check to function in their job.

What they didn't know was how we processed things after we got home. How the sights, smells, and screams haunted our dreams and sometimes affected our relationships.

CHAPTER 44

Chocolate Pies

I was to see the complainant about a theft from his yard. It was late in the evening. All the other houses on the street had short front yards with the obligatory bushes and flowers. The victim's home was behind a sold wall of 20-foot-high arborvitae. A narrow rectangle had been cut in its center to allow entry. I had driven by the place on routine patrol and was always curious about the tiny house I could see through the rectangle.

I opened the gate and proceeded down the long, dark walkway, the house a good hundred feet farther back from the street than all the others in the neighborhood. The yard had been neglected.

The door opened after the third time I knocked. The elderly man personified the Mother Goose rhyme, "There was a crooked man who... [lived] in a crooked house." His back was bent terribly, and his frozen neck didn't allow him to angle his head up enough to look me in the face. He invited me in.

Only a weak dangling lightbulb over a cluttered kitchen table barely illuminated the place, leaving everything out of its radius in shadow. I no longer remember what was stolen, other than it was something minor, but I do remember the man—and his eating habits.

His date of birth said he was 95, his body cruelly twisted by the years or perhaps beaten down by a life of hard work. Or life itself. He said his wife was long dead, and it was evident by the look of the place he had been a bachelor for years.

There were lots and lots of empty boxes that had held frozen chocolate pies, the kind found in supermarkets. There were multiple stacks on the kitchen table, the counters, atop the refrigerator, and by the garbage can. Forks, their tines brown, rested across chocolate smeared dirty plates.

I like chocolate pie, but this man LIKED chocolate pie.

There was no indication of any other food in the place; it was just empty chocolate pie boxes and nothing else. I could only assume his refrigerator and freezer were stacked with them too, ready for breakfast, lunch, dinner, and in-between snacks. It bothered me that this man nearing the century mark was eating so poorly.

But then, why not?

He was a sweet man, and we had a friendly chat after I got information for his report.

A couple of months later, a for-sale sign was speared into the ground in front of the tall arborvitae. I asked a neighbor out raking leaves what I already assumed.

The man had died a few weeks earlier.

I had the honor of meeting so many elderly people on the job, all of them with a story. Some had been teachers, World War II veterans, hard-working laborers, mothers, fathers, and grandparents.

I remember being in a 90-year-old woman's home taking a report on something. I noticed several old black and white photographs of a beautiful young woman dancing ballet on a stage. "Is this you?" I asked.

"It is!" she answered with a burst of enthusiasm. She went on to tell me of her years as a top ballerina in the American Ballet Theater in New York City.

Too many elderly men and women I met lived alone, undoubtedly passing on without anyone knowing their life story.

My dad died two days after his 98th birthday. There was a Ritter Sport Milk Chocolate Bar with hazelnuts I had given him for his birthday still on his nightstand, unopened. It was his favorite. He told many stories of his life in the 1920s, about the Great Depression, World War II, and when he met my mom. Still, I wish I would have asked him more about his life and written it down.

Writer Ray Bradbury said, "Old men only lie in wait for people to ask them to talk. Then they rattle on like a rusty elevator wheezing up a shaft." To this, I say two things: It's not true of every old man. Even when it is, so what? Just shut up and listen to them as there is a world of lessons and truths to be heard.

I wish I had met the bent old man who lived in the tiny house sooner. I would have stopped in once a week carrying two cups of coffee and hit him up for a piece of chocolate pie. And to hear a story.

CONCLUSION

A salute those special people who work every day with the dead.

The Morgue

The County Morgue was in one of my regular patrol beats. They have since moved to a new and improved location. When I patrolled the old area, the deceased was taken to the brick building with a front entrance for the living and a rear drive-up for the vans. Visitors would enter a pleasant office with multiple desks and friendly office staff. A heavy-looking door led to a foyer of sorts on the right-back wall, the space several degrees colder than the outer office. Another set of heavy doors opened to an assortment of workrooms where bodies were processed and stored. That room was chillier.

As explained earlier, I lost my sense of smell for several years while I was on the job, a blessing and a curse. Before that happened, I would say the morgue smelled like a hospital: a vague chemical blend of cleansers, embalming fluid, and an assortment of substances used in ME's work. And it smelled like the dead.

Here a morgue manager describes her experience with the odors. Marieclaire.com, "What it's like to work in a morgue." I'm paraphrasing.

When a body arrives, we remove the organs with scalpels so a pathologist can do an autopsy. After the cause of death is determined, we put the organs back. If the deceased is disfigured, we try to reconstruct the body.

On TV and in the movies, actors never get a speck of blood on them. But that's not real. The job is bloody, and the smell is revolting, rotten but sweet. After 10 minutes, your nose adjusts, and the gag reflex subsides. Sometimes it takes half a day and multiple showers to get the smell off.

On Coronertalk.com, "Controlling Odor," one person said, "A dead body, specifically a human corpse has a rank and pungent smell mixed with a tinge of sickening sweetness. Imagine a rotting piece of meat with a couple drops of cheap perfume, and you're halfway to understanding what a human corpse smells like."

So visiting the morgue was one of the times my lack of smell was a blessing.

My partner and I got to know many medical examiners. They were all highly professional and compassionate to friends and family during body retrievals. When a situation out in the field became tense with angry people and those out of control with grief, the MEs always obeyed our requests to stay back until we got the scene under control.

Sometimes when we stopped in at the morgue for coffee, we'd get asked to go in the back with them to see if we recognized a John or Jane Doe they had gotten in. On one occasion, they had picked up a young woman left on a garbage heap. Her skimpy attire, heavy makeup, and spiked heels suggested a prostitute, as did the area where she was found. We didn't recognize her.

So that we had a photo to show around, the ME retrieved a Polaroid camera. He handed it to me. "You snap, and I'll open her eyes." I leaned against the gurney and stretched out over her head as far as I could without collapsing across her torso.

But the task wasn't easy with this woman because every time the ME opened her eyes, they snapped closed.

"Okay," he said, "get in position to take the shot. On the count of two, I'll open her eyes, and on three, I'll jerk my hands away, and you take it." It still took us three tries before we got a good pic, though he had stretched her lids so wide it made her look shocked.

We returned to the street and cruised up to a few working girls to show the photo. By the fifth one, we had a name. Not long after, the detectives arrested her killer.

After nearly a year of patrolling that beat where there were so many dead body calls, where we routinely worked with medical examiners, took coffee breaks with them, and sometimes watched autopsies, I began to see the faces of the dead away from the job. I'd be talking to my neighbor over the fence, and I'd unexpectedly superimpose my most recent dead person's face over his. This usually happened when the live person's expression was like a frozen one that I'd recently seen on a deceased face.

When it began occurring when talking to my family, I knew I needed a break. I told my partner I'd like to limit our trips to the morgue to only those times when dispatch sent us there. He quickly agreed since he had been having issues as well.

Does it bother medical examiners too? It probably depends on the examiner. Most likely, people who go into that line of work aren't disturbed by the sights and sounds. One worker said there was nothing to get used to because it didn't bother him even when he was new.

Another ME said that it was essential not to be sensitive to terrible smells, insects of every breed crawling on the body, and workers. She added that MEs must take every precaution when handling the dead since some might have infectious diseases, such as AIDS, Hepatitis, and others.

For sure, medical examiners and other morgue employees are a special breed, and we thank them for what they do.

Through a Small Funeral Parlor Window

My friend JT grew up in a funeral home in a small town east of Portland. His dad had been its director. The father was a caring man who often took garden vegetables, old TVs, and lawnmowers from low-income people in exchange for services. When JT grew up and married, he and his wife bought a house next door to the funeral home.

One warm summer night, JT and I were sitting on his back porch, knocking back a beer or two and swapping lies. At one point, a hearse pulled into the funeral home's driveway, which we could easily see from where we sat. The driver activated the garage door opener, the hearse backed in, and the big door returned to the down position.

"Are they bringing one in?" I asked JT.

He took a pull from his beer. "Sometimes two or three a night." He nodded toward a small window on the second floor. "Watch up there."

The window, just off the upper left corner of the garage door, was dark. If the body was going up there, I thought, there must be a ramp or an elevator.

A bright white light abruptly filled the square, revealing a back wall with something that looked like a white neck strap hanging from a hook. A large unlit light with a chrome hood protruded from the left side of the window. "Processing room?" I asked. JT nodded.

The top of a man's head came into view, balding on top, gray on the sides. The window was high enough that his shoulders were out of sight below the bottom frame. "That your dad?" I'd met him, but I couldn't see enough of the man in the window to know for sure.

"That's Allen. He's worked for dad for a long time." JT stood, saying he needed to go kiss his daughter goodnight. "Keep watching the window show and see if you can figure out what's going on."

A moment after he left, Allen's head turned toward the wall. A hand appeared from the bottom of the window frame, reached up to the hook, and lifted the neck strap from it. When it was raised high enough to clear the hanger, I could see it was part of a white apron. Another hand appeared, and the two slipped it over the balding head.

Allen's head moved out of the right frame for a moment before it reappeared in the window, backing up. He's pulling the gurney into place, I guessed. A hand reached up to the domed light, turning on its brilliance. It adjusted the angle to better illuminate whatever he was going to do. Allen's head angled forward then straightened. Unzipping the body bag?

A hand reached out of the left side of the frame, then reappeared, pulling something that looked like a clear tube. Time for the embalming, I thought.

For the next few minutes, Allen's head moved in and out of frame several times. When I could see him, he seemed to be manipulating something. Maybe adjusting the body, the embalming device, or doing some function unknown to me.

JT returned with fresh brews and sat back down. I told him I thought Allen was embalming the person. He nodded. "There's nothing like the smell of embalming fluid in the evening," he said. We chatted about other things as I continued to watch the window.

Nearly an hour passed before Allen's hand moved the embalming tube out of the left window frame. It reached up and switched off the hanging work light. The room was less brilliant now, signifying at least part of his job with the deceased was over.

Allen's head disappeared out of the right frame, perhaps to retrieve something. He backed into the room, stopping just short of the left window frame. His shoulders lifted, then his forearms floated up from the bottom of the frame, followed by his hands. They were gripping the ends of a white sheet; they made a flipping motion. The sheet billowed upward, then drifted out of sight below the bottom of the window.

The body was draped.

Hands lifted the apron from around his neck and slipped the strap back over the hook.

Allen moved around the room for a minute, doing whatever final tasks I couldn't decipher, then moved out of frame. The window went dark.

I looked at JT without saying anything. I wasn't sure what I was feeling. I needed time to process it.

"A funeral director's job is one of the most unappreciated professions there is," he said. "But it's one of the most valuable ones in our culture."

I once saw a computer mouse pad on a homicide detective's desk that read, "Our day begins when yours ends."

The same can be said for medical examiners and funeral home people.

ABOUT THE AUTHOR

Loren W. Christensen has been involved in law enforcement since 1967. He began as a 21-year-old military policeman in the U.S. Army, serving stateside and as a patrolman in Saigon, Vietnam during the war. At 26, he joined the Portland, Oregon Police Bureau working a variety of jobs to include street patrol, gang enforcement, intelligence, bodyguarding, and academy trainer, retiring after 25 years.

In 1997, Loren began a full-time career as a writer, now with nearly 60 books in print with seven publishers, as well as magazine articles and blog pieces. He edited a police newspaper for seven years. His non-fiction includes books on martial arts, police work, PTSD, mental preparation for violence, meditation, nutrition, exercise, and various subcultures, to include prostitution, street gangs, skid row, and the warrior community.

His fiction series *Dukkha* was a finalist in the prestigious USA Best Book Awards. He has also written novellas, nearly a dozen short stories, and several omnibuses.

As a martial arts student and teacher since 1965, Loren has earned a 1st-dan black belt in the Filipino fighting art of *arnis,* a 2nd-degree black belt in *aiki jujitsu and, on* October 23, 2018, the American Karate Black Belt Association in Texas, awarded him a 10th-dan black belt in karate. Loren was inducted into the master's Hall of Fame in 2011.

OTHER TITLES BY LOREN W. CHRISTENSEN

The following are available on Amazon, from their publishers, and through the usual book outlets. Signed copies can be purchased at LWC Books, www.lwcbooks.com

Street Stoppers
Fighting In The Clinch
Fighter's Fact Book
Fighter's Fact Book 2
Solo Training **(Bestseller)**
Solo Training 2
Solo Training 3
Speed Training
The Fighter's Body
Total Defense
The Mental Edge
The Way Alone
Far Beyond Defensive Tactics
Fighting Power
Crouching Tiger
Anything Goes
Winning With American Kata
Total Defense
Riot
Warriors
On Combat **(Bestseller)**
Warrior Mindset
Deadly Force Encounters
Deadly Force Encounters, Second Edition
Surviving Workplace Violence
Surviving A School Shooting
Gangbangers
Skinhead Street Gangs
Hookers, Tricks And Cops
Way Of The Warrior

Skid Row Beat
Defensive Tactics
Missing Children
Fight Back: Self-Defense For Women
Extreme Joint Locking
Timing In The Martial Arts
Fighter's Guide to Hard-Core Heavy Bag Training
The Brutal Art Of Ripping, Poking And Pressing Vital Targets
How To Live Safely In A Dangerous World
Fighting The Pain Resistant Attacker
Evolution Of Weaponry
Meditation For Warriors
Mental Rehearsal For Warriors
Prostate Cancer
Cops' True Stories Of The Paranormal **(Bestseller)**
Seekers of the Paranormal
Policing Saigon
Musings on Violence
Street Lessons, A Journey
Dead Body Calls

Fiction

Dukkha: The Suffering **(Best Books Award Finalist)**
Dukkha: Reverb
Dukkha: Unloaded
Dukkha: Hungry Ghosts
Old Ed, Omnibus
Boss, Omnibus
Knife Fighter, Omnibus
The Reincarnation of Kato the Monk, novella
The Life and Death of Sensei, novella
Close Encounters of the Seventh Kind, novella

Short Story Fiction

Old Ed
Old Ed 2
Old Ed 3
Old Ed 4
Old Ed 5
Parts
Knife Fighter
Knife Fighter 2, novella
Boss
Boss 2
Boss 3

DVDs

Solo Training
Fighting Dirty
Speed Training
Masters And Styles
Vital Targets
The Brutal Art Of Ripping, And Pressing Vital Targets

Note: On Combat and Policing Saigon are also available in audio from Amazon

You might also like. All are available on Amazon

COPS' TRUE STORIES

of the PARANORMAL

GHOSTS, UFOS, and OTHER SHIVERS

Loren W.
CHRISTENSEN

BEST-SELLING COAUTHOR OF *ON COMBAT*

DEADLY FORCE
ENCOUNTERS

SECOND EDITION

COPS & CITIZENS DEFENDING
THEMSELVES AND OTHERS

WIN THE FIGHT
WIN THE AFTERMATH

ALEXIS ARTWOHL PhD
LOREN W CHRISTENSEN

LT. COL. DAVE GROSSMAN
AND LOREN W. CHRISTENSEN
ON COMBAT
FOURTH EDITION
The Psychology and Physiology of Deadly Conflict
in War and Peace

POLICING SAIGON

"Amazing and powerful..."

"Veterans of Vietnam, and of today's wars, will see themselves in this book and know they are not alone."
Lt. Col. Dave Grossman

Loren W. CHRISTENSEN
co-author of *On Combat*

Printed in Great Britain
by Amazon

18652338R00139